Good Housekeeping Favorite Recipes
Cookies!

Good Housekeeping Favorite Recipes

Cookies!

HEARST BOOKS

A DIVISION OF STERLING PUBLISHING CO., INC.

NEW YORK

GOOD HOUSEKEEPING
Ellen Levine   Editor in Chief
Susan Westmoreland   Food Director
Susan Deborah Goldsmith   Associate Food Director
Delia Hammock   Nutrition Director
Sharon Franke   Food Appliances Director
Richard Eisenberg   Special Projects Director
Marilu Lopez   Art Director

Book Design by Renato Stanisic

Library of Congress Cataloging-in-Publication Data
Cookies! : favorite Good Housekeeping recipes.
        p.cm.
    Includes index.
    ISBN 1-58816-276-1
1. Cookies. I. Good housekeeping.
    TX772.C6558 2004
  641.8'654--dc22   2003021002

    12 11 10 9 8 7 6 5 4

Published by Hearst Books
A Division of Sterling Publishing Co., Inc.
387 Park Avenue South, New York, NY 10016

Good Housekeeping is a trademark owned by Hearst Magazines Property, Inc., in USA, and Hearst Communications, Inc., in Canada. Hearst Books is a trademark owned by Hearst Communications, Inc.

The Good Housekeeping Cookbook Seal guarantees that the recipes in this cookbook meet the strict standards of the Good Housekeeping Institute, a source of reliable information and a consumer advocate since 1900. Every recipe has been triple-tested for ease, reliability, and great taste.

www.goodhousekeeping.com

Distributed in Canada by Sterling Publishing
c/o Canadian Manda Group, 165 Dufferin Street,
Toronto, Ontario, Canada M6K 3H6

Distributed in Australia by Capricorn Link (Australia) Pty. Ltd.
P.O. Box 704, Windsor, NSW 2756 Australia

Printed in China

ISBN 1-58816-276-1

For information about custom editions, special sales, premium and coporate purchases, please contact Sterling Special Sales Department at 800-805-5489 or specialsales@sterlingpub.com

CONTENTS

FOREWORD

Welcome to Good Housekeeping Cookies

Whether you are an experienced cookie baker or a novice preparing to bake your first batch, you are about to discover how simple and satisfying cookie baking can be. Just the aroma of cookies baking, whether they are plain or fancy, trendy or traditional, brings out a smile from anyone who passes by. In our test kitchens at *Good Housekeeping*, whenever we bake cookies, the rest of the magazine staff stops in more frequently than usual. We always reward them with a taste of whatever we are baking, and in return many of them have shared with us their family's favorite cookie recipes.

The recipes that follow have been selected from the many hundreds in the *Good Housekeeping* collection. Most were developed in our test kitchens, some have come from staff, and some from readers, but all have been triple tested (and staff tasted), so we know they are good. We hope that the time you spend baking recipes from *Cookies!* will leave you with many warm, wonderful, kitchen memories.

Susan Westmoreland
Food Director,
Good Housekeeping

PERFECT COOKIES EVERY TIME

What smells better than a batch of cookies hot from the oven? Better yet, is when they turn out just the way you want them—moist and chewy, or light and crispy—never burned or dried out. And getting it right is easy if you follow the step-by-step directions that come with every recipe and use the ingredients called for.

Most cookies don't require any fancy equipment. However, there are a few essential baking utensils that can make the difference between a cookie that tastes just so-so and one that makes folks say *Wow—these are great!* So before you start baking, it's a good idea to make sure you have the right equipment on hand and that you're using the best ingredients.

Measure By Measure

The primary reason cookies don't turn out quite right is usually failure to measure ingredients properly. More than any other form of cooking, baking requires very precise measurements. Even though it worked for Grandma, don't use coffee or tea cups,

Front: Standard dry measuring cups and spoons; Back: 1-, 2-, and 4-cup glass measuring cups

or tableware teaspoons and tablespoons for measuring. Ideally, you should have:

- set of standard dry measuring cups
- set of standard measuring spoons
- spatula for leveling them
- 1-cup glass measure for liquids
- 2-cup and 4-cup glass measures for liquids (if possible).

The Right Cookie Sheets

High-quality cookie sheets and baking pans are the second most important secret to perfect cookies. You should use heavy-gauge metal sheets and pans with a dull finish—aluminum is ideal. These double-thick insulated cookie sheets and baking pans will help prevent your cookies from getting extra-dark bottoms. Avoid dark cookie sheets—they can blacken the bottoms of cookies because they absorb more heat. If your cookie sheets are old and discolored, you can line them with foil to help deflect the heat.

Size is important too. Cookie sheets should be at least 2 inches smaller in length and width than your oven so that air can circulate freely around them. So measure your oven before you buy new cookie sheets. If possible buy rimless sheets, or those with only one or two edges turned. They will also help air to circulate around the cookies.

Mixing It Up

While a lot of cookie batters can be stirred up with whatever spoon is on hand, the right equipment makes it easier, particularly if your recipe calls for chopping a lot of nuts or doing a lot of mixing. You should have:

- stand mixer or hand beater
- food processor or mini-processor
- set of mixing bowls: small, medium, and large
- several wooden spoons for stirring hot ingredients on the stove

Timing Is Everything

One of the most common mistakes is not timing the baking properly, which results in burned or underdone cookies. Fortunately this problem is easily avoided. Buy a good oven thermometer and check it closely to make sure your oven is at the correct temperature before you start baking. It's also wise to start checking your cookies a couple of minutes before they're supposed to be done. So get a kitchen timer and set it a few minutes early.

Cool Ideas
To remove the hot cookie sheets from the oven safely, you will need two sturdy potholders. A cake tester is great for testing bar cookies for doneness and a good investment if you don't have one. Next, you'll need racks on which to set the baking sheets while the cookies cool. Never set a hot sheet on the counter.

Into the Cookie Jar
When the cookies are cool, you'll want to store them so they stay nice and crisp—or chewy—as the case may be. You can use either a tin or a jar, as long as it has a tight-fitting cover.

Specialty Cookie Equipment
Baking supply shops have enough cookie-making tools to fill all the shelves in your kitchen, and it would be fun to have them all. But you don't need them. You can bake every recipe in this book with just a few additional utensils:

- cookie cutters of various shapes
- cookie press for molded cookies
- cookie scoops
- grater
- juicer
- parchment paper
- pastry bag and large tips
- pastry brush
- pastry cloth
- pastry wheel
- rolling pin and pin cover
- ruler
- wire whisk
- yeast thermometer

The Ingredients of Success

Baking is a precise art. To ensure that your cookies will taste delicious and have just the right texture, it is important to use the exact ingredients called for and handle them properly.

• *Butter or margarine?* While either one may be used for many cookie recipes, for the best flavor and texture, use butter. If you prefer to use margarine, make sure it contains 80 percent fat. Don't substitute light margarine, vegetable-oil spreads, or whipped butters for stick margarine; they contain more water than standard sticks and won't work in cookies unless the recipes have been formulated especially for the products.

• *To soften butter or margarine,* let it stand, wrapped on a counter or unwrapped in a mixing bowl, at room temperature for an hour. You can speed up the process by cutting it into small pieces first. It's best not to soften butter or margarine in the microwave. The microwave can melt some areas, which can hurt the cookies' texture.

• *To grease cookie sheets,* your best bet is vegetable shortening. Avoid both butter, which browns, and vegetable oil, which leaves a gummy residue on baking pans. Grease cookie sheets only when a recipe directs you to. Some cookies have a high fat content, so greasing isn't necessary.

• *The type of flour is important.* Most cookie recipes call for all-purpose flour. Occasionally, a cookie recipe will call for cake flour, which is higher in starch and will produce a more tender cookie. Cake and all-purpose flours are not interchangeable, so read your recipe carefully. In either case, make sure the flour you are using is *not* self-rising.

• *Baking soda* is a leavening agent which makes cookies rise. Keep the box or tin tightly closed in a cool, dry place so the baking soda stays very active. For best results, replace after six months if you haven't used it up.

• *Baking powder* is a premeasured mixture of baking soda and an acid. (It takes twice as much baking powder as baking soda to leaven a product.) Again, keep baking powder tightly closed in a cool, dry place and for best results, replace after six months.

The Way to Measure

To get the same results every time you make a recipe, it is important to use standard measuring equipment and to measure carefully.

• *Always* use standard measuring spoons to measure both liquid and dry ingredients. For convenience, measure the dry ingredients first.

• *Never* use dry-ingredient cups to measure liquid ingredients or liquid-ingredient cups to measure dry ingredients.

• *Always* measure ingredients over waxed paper or into an empty bowl but *never* over your bowl of already measured ingredients—just in case there is a spill.

• *Liquids.* Use clear glass measuring cups. Place the cup on a level surface and bend down so that your eyes are in line with the marks on the cup.

• *Dry ingredients.* To measure flour and other dry ingredients that tend to pack down in the storage container, stir and then spoon them into a standard dry-ingredient measuring cup. Level the top surface with a spatula, scraping off the excess into a bowl.

• *Granulated sugar.* Just scoop or pour it into a dry-ingredient measuring cup.

• *Brown sugar.* Pack it into the measuring cup and then level.

• *Butter, vegetable shortening, and margarine.* Tablespoons are marked on the wrapper, so you can just cut off the desired amount using a knife.

• *Syrup, honey,* and other sticky ingredients. Lightly oil the cup first and the ingredient will pour right out without sticking to the cup.

Now perfectly equipped, with the right ingredients on hand, you're ready to bake fabulous cookies!

Stir the flour and spoon it into a standard dry measuring cup to keep it from packing.

Level the top of the dry measure by passing a metal spatula over the top to remove excess.

BAR COOKIES

From brownies and blondies to fruit-and-nut squares, bar cookies are not only delicious but also the easiest of all cookies to make. Many of these tempting bars don't even require an electric mixer—you can just stir the batter with a spoon, pat or pour it into a pan, and pop it into the oven.

They are the perfect family dessert: You can mix them up quickly and let them bake while you are preparing the rest of the meal. Then serve them warm from the oven. They make delectable company fare too, especially when topped with ice cream or whipped cream. And because these scrumptious cookies travel well—you can transport them right in their baking pan—they're an easy bring-along for picnics, parties, and bake sales.

For great bar cookies every time, be sure to:

• *Follow recipe storage directions.* Because bar cookies are likely to be softer and moister than many other cookies, it is very important to store them properly.

• *Cool bar cookies completely* in the pan before cutting them, then store them in their baking pan, tightly covered with foil or plastic wrap.

• *Store cakelike cookies* that don't contain perishable ingredients in a tight cookie jar or tin in a cool spot in your kitchen for up to three days. Be sure to add a slice of bread or apple to keep them moist and change it every other day to keep it from molding.

• *Refrigerate any cookies* that contain perishable ingredients, such as eggs and cream, and use them within several days. These would include lemon bars, any cheesecake-type cookies, and any cookies with custard or cream fillings.

• *To freeze cookies,* wrap them tightly first. They will keep well frozen for up to a month. You might want to wrap bars individually for freezing so they are ready to pack into box lunches. You don't need to thaw them, they will keep other foods cool as they thaw. Or you can warm them briefly in a microwave or toaster oven for a snack.

Chocolate-Swirl Peanut Butter Blondies

You can drop the chocolate and peanut butter doughs in a patchwork on the peanut butter base or swirl a knife through them for a marbled effect.

PREP: 20 MINUTES   BAKE: 25 MINUTES
MAKES 24 BLONDIES

2 1/2 cups all-purpose flour
1 1/2 teaspoons baking powder
1/2 teaspoon salt
3 squares (3 ounces) semisweet chocolate, chopped
1 square (1 ounce) unsweetened chocolate, chopped
1 cup creamy peanut butter

1/2 cup butter or margarine (1 stick), softened
1 3/4 cups packed light brown sugar
3 large eggs
2 teaspoons vanilla extract
1 package (6 ounces) semisweet chocolate chips (1 cup)

1. Preheat oven to 350°F. In medium bowl, combine flour, baking powder, and salt. In heavy 1-quart saucepan, melt semisweet and unsweetened chocolates, stirring frequently, until smooth. Set aside.

2. In large bowl, with mixer at medium speed, beat peanut butter, butter, and brown sugar until light and fluffy, about 2 minutes. Add eggs and vanilla; beat until blended. Reduce speed to low; beat in flour mixture just until blended (dough will be stiff).

3. Place one-third of dough (about 1 3/4 cups) in separate large bowl. Stir in melted chocolate until blended; stir in 3/4 cup chocolate chips.

4. With hand, pat half of remaining plain peanut butter dough onto bottom of ungreased 13" by 9" baking pan to form thin layer. In random pattern, drop chocolate dough and remaining plain peanut butter dough on top of peanut butter layer; lightly pat. Sprinkle remaining 1/4 cup chocolate chips on top.

5. Bake until toothpick inserted in center comes out clean, 25 to 30 minutes. Cool completely in pan on wire rack.

6. When cool, cut lengthwise into 4 strips, then cut each strip crosswise into 6 pieces.

Each blondie: About 273 calories, 6 g protein, 34 g carbohydrate, 14 g total fat (6 g saturated), 37 mg cholesterol, 184 mg sodium.

Almond Cheesecake Brownies

In this updated classic, two kinds of chocolate and a swirl of almond-flavored cheesecake bake to decadent perfection. For the best flavor use bar cream cheese, not whipped.

PREP: 30 MINUTES   BAKE: 35 MINUTES
MAKES 24 BROWNIES

1 1/4 cups all-purpose flour
3/4 teaspoon baking powder
1/2 teaspoon salt
1/2 cup butter or margarine (1 stick)
4 squares (4 ounces) unsweetened
  chocolate, chopped
4 squares (4 ounces) semisweet
  chocolate, chopped

2 cups sugar
5 large eggs
2 1/2 teaspoons vanilla extract
1 1/2 packages (8 ounces each) cream
  cheese
3/4 teaspoon almond extract

1. Preheat oven to 350°F. Grease 13" by 9" baking pan. In small bowl, combine flour, baking powder, and salt.

2. In heavy 4-quart saucepan, melt butter and unsweetened and semisweet chocolates over low heat, stirring, until smooth. Remove from heat. With wooden spoon, beat in 1 1/2 cups sugar. Add 4 eggs and 2 teaspoons vanilla; beat until well blended. Stir in flour mixture just until blended.

3. In small bowl, with mixer at medium speed, beat cream cheese until smooth; gradually beat in remaining 1/2 cup sugar. Beat in remaining egg, almond extract, and remaining 1/2 teaspoon vanilla just until blended.

4. Spread 1 1/2 cups chocolate batter in prepared pan. Spoon cream cheese mixture in 6 large dollops on top of chocolate mixture (cream cheese mixture will cover most of chocolate batter). Spoon remaining chocolate batter over and between cream cheese in 6 large dollops. With tip of knife, cut and twist through mixtures to create marbled effect.

5. Bake until toothpick inserted in center comes out almost clean, 35 to 40 minutes. Cool completely in pan on wire rack.

6. When cool, cut lengthwise into 4 strips, then cut each strip crosswise into 6 pieces.

Each brownie: About 238 calories, 4 g protein, 26 g carbohydrate, 14 g total fat (8 g saturated), 70 mg cholesterol, 159 mg sodium.

MARBLING BROWNIE BATTER

To produce a marbled effect with two different-colored batters, pull and swirl a kitchen knife through the batters.

Almond Shortbread Brownies

A layer of rich chocolate ganache covers this party-size pan of triple-layered chocolate shortbread bars. We lined the pan with foil, which makes it easier to lift them out of the pan and cut them without breaking.

PREP: 1 HOUR PLUS COOLING   BAKE: 40 MINUTES
MAKES 72 BROWNIES

1 cup whole natural almonds
(4 ounces), toasted (see page 73)
3/4 cup confectioners' sugar
1 3/4 cups butter or margarine
(3 1/2 sticks), softened
2 3/4 cups all-purpose flour
1/4 teaspoon almond extract
5 squares (5 ounces) unsweetened
chocolate, chopped

3 large eggs
2 cups granulated sugar
1/4 teaspoon salt
2 teaspoons vanilla extract
6 squares (6 ounces) semisweet
chocolate, chopped
1/3 cup heavy or whipping cream
1/2 cup sliced almonds, toasted
(see page 73)

1. Preheat oven to 350°F. Line 15 1/2" by 10 1/2" jelly-roll pan with foil, extending foil over rim.

2. In blender or in food processor with knife blade attached, process whole almonds with 1/4 cup confectioners' sugar until nuts are finely ground.

3. In large bowl, with mixer at low speed, beat 3/4 cup butter and remaining 1/2 cup confectioners' sugar until blended. Increase speed to high and beat mixture until light and fluffy. Reduce speed to low; beat in ground-almond mixture, 1 3/4 cups flour, and almond extract just until blended (dough will be stiff). With hands, pat dough onto bottom of prepared pan.

4. Bake until golden, 20 to 25 minutes. Cool in pan on wire rack.

5. Meanwhile, in heavy 2-quart saucepan, melt unsweetened chocolate and remaining 1 cup butter over low heat, stirring frequently, until smooth. Remove from heat. Cool slightly, about 10 minutes.

6. In large bowl, with mixer at high speed, beat eggs, granulated sugar, salt, and 1 teaspoon vanilla until ribbon forms when beaters are lifted, 5 to 10 minutes. Beat in cooled chocolate mixture until blended. With wooden spoon, stir in remaining 1 cup flour. Pour chocolate-flour mixture over cooled shortbread crust. Bake until toothpick inserted 1 inch from edge comes out almost clean, 20 to 25 minutes. Cool in pan on wire rack.

7. In heavy 2-quart saucepan, melt semisweet chocolate and cream over low heat, stirring frequently until smooth. Remove from heat; stir in remaining 1 teaspoon vanilla. Lift foil with brownies out of pan and place on cutting board; peel foil away from sides. With small metal spatula, spread chocolate glaze over brownie. Sprinkle almond slices over top. Let stand at room temperature until set, about 2 hours, or refrigerate 30 minutes.

8. When set, cut lengthwise into 6 strips, then cut each strip crosswise into 12 pieces.

Each brownie: About 127 calories, 2 g protein, 13 g carbohydrate, 8 g total fat (4 g saturated), 22 mg cholesterol, 57 mg sodium.

BEATING EGGS TO A RIBBON

Whole eggs have been beaten sufficiently if a ribbon forms when the beaters are lifted.

Fudgy Low-Fat Brownies

Corn syrup keeps these coffee-flavored cocoa brownies so moist and tender no one will ever notice that they are low in fat.

PREP: 15 MINUTES   BAKE: 18 MINUTES
MAKES 16 BROWNIES

1 teaspoon instant espresso-coffee powder	1/4 teaspoon salt
	3 tablespoons butter or margarine
1 teaspoon hot water	3/4 cup sugar
3/4 cup all-purpose flour	2 large egg whites
1/2 cup unsweetened cocoa	1/4 cup dark corn syrup
1/2 teaspoon baking powder	1 teaspoon vanilla extract

1. Preheat oven to 350°F. Grease 8-inch square baking pan. In cup, dissolve espresso powder in hot water; set aside. In large bowl, combine flour, cocoa, baking powder, and salt.

2. In 2-quart saucepan, melt butter over low heat. Remove from heat. With wooden spoon, stir in sugar, egg whites, corn syrup, espresso, and vanilla until blended. Stir sugar mixture into flour mixture just until blended (do not overmix). Pour batter into prepared pan.

3. Bake until toothpick inserted in center comes out almost clean, 18 to 22 minutes. Cool brownies completely in pan on wire rack.

4. When cool, cut brownies into 4 strips, then cut each strip crosswise into 4 pieces. If brownies are difficult to cut, use knife dipped in hot water and dried; repeat as necessary.

Each brownie: About 103 calories, 2 g protein, 19 g carbohydrate, 3 g total fat (2 g saturated), 6 mg cholesterol, 88 mg sodium.

Pennsylvania-Dutch Brownies

Good Housekeeping reader Yvonne D. Kanoff of Mount Joy, Pennsylvania, lives in chocolate country and just couldn't resist adding some of the local product to her spice bars. The delicious spiced brownies that resulted will make you wonder why we haven't all been doing it for years.

PREP: 20 MINUTES PLUS COOLING   BAKE: 15 MINUTES
MAKES 30 BROWNIES

4 tablespoons butter or margarine	1 cup plus 2 teaspoons sugar
1 square (1 ounce) unsweetened	1 1/8 teaspoons ground cinnamon
chocolate	1 teaspoon ground ginger
1/4 cup light molasses	1/2 teaspoon ground cloves
2 large eggs	1/2 teaspoon baking soda
1 1/2 cups all-purpose flour	1/2 teaspoon salt

1. Preheat oven to 375°F. Grease 13" by 9" baking pan.

2. In 4-quart saucepan, melt butter and chocolate over low heat. Remove from heat.

3. With wire whisk or fork, stir in molasses, then eggs. With spoon, stir in flour, 1 cup sugar, 1 teaspoon cinnamon, ginger, cloves, baking soda, and salt just until blended. Spread batter evenly in pan. Bake until toothpick inserted 2 inches from edge comes out clean, 15 to 20 minutes.

4. Meanwhile, in cup, combine remaining 2 teaspoons sugar and remaining 1/8 teaspoon cinnamon; set aside.

5. Remove pan from oven; immediately sprinkle brownies with cinnamon-sugar mixture. Cool brownies in pan on wire rack at least 2 hours.

6. When cool, cut brownies lengthwise into 3 strips, then cut each strip crosswise into 5 pieces. Cut each piece diagonally in half.

Each brownie: About 80 calories, 1 g protein, 14 g carbohydrate, 2 g total fat (1 g saturated), 14 mg cholesterol, 80 mg sodium.

Cocoa Brownies

You need only a small bowl, a saucepan, and a spoon to assemble these easy brownies. And they're done in just thirty-five minutes—start to finish!

PREP: 10 MINUTES   BAKE: 25 MINUTES

MAKES 16 BROWNIES

1/2 cup all-purpose flour	1 cup sugar
1/2 cup unsweetened cocoa	2 large eggs
1/4 teaspoon baking powder	1 teaspoon vanilla extract
1/4 teaspoon salt	1 cup walnuts (4 ounces),
1/2 cup butter or margarine (1 stick)	coarsely chopped (optional)

1. Preheat oven to 350°F. Grease 9-inch square baking pan. In bowl, combine flour, cocoa, baking powder, and salt.

2. In 3-quart saucepan, melt butter over low heat. Remove from heat and stir in sugar. Stir in eggs, one at a time, until well blended; add vanilla. Stir flour mixture into sugar mixture until blended. Stir in nuts, if using. Spread batter evenly in prepared pan.

3. Bake until toothpick inserted 2 inches from center comes out almost clean, about 25 minutes. Cool completely in pan on wire rack.

4. When cool, cut into 4 strips, then cut each strip crosswise into 4 pieces.

Each brownie: About 132 calories, 2 g protein, 17 g carbohydrate, 7 g total fat (4 g saturated), 42 mg cholesterol, 110 mg sodium.

LINING PAN WITH FOIL

Turn the baking pan bottom side up. Cover the pan tightly with foil, shiny side out. Remove foil cover.

Turn the baking pan right side up and carefully fit the molded foil into it, smoothing foil to fit into the edges.

Fudgy Brownies with Praline Topping

Fudgy Brownies

These moist chocolate brownies have been a *Good Housekeeping* tradition for many years. You can serve them plain or add the Praline Topping for an over-the-top presentation.

PREP: 10 MINUTES   BAKE: 30 MINUTES
MAKES 24 BROWNIES

1 1/4 cups all-purpose flour	4 squares (4 ounces) semisweet
1/2 teaspoon salt	chocolate, chopped
3/4 cup butter or margarine	2 cups sugar
(1 1/2 sticks)	1 tablespoon vanilla extract
4 squares (4 ounces) unsweetened	5 large eggs, beaten
chocolate, chopped	Praline Topping (optional; recipe follows)

1. Preheat oven to 350°F. Grease 13" by 9" baking pan. In small bowl, combine flour and salt.

2. In heavy 4-quart saucepan, melt butter and unsweetened and semisweet chocolates over low heat, stirring frequently, until smooth. Remove from heat. With wooden spoon, stir in sugar and vanilla. Add eggs; stir until well mixed. Stir flour mixture into chocolate mixture just until blended. Spread batter evenly in prepared pan.

3. Bake until toothpick inserted 1 inch from edge comes out clean, about 30 minutes. Cool completely in pan on wire rack.

4. When cool, cut lengthwise into 4 strips, then cut each strip crosswise into 6 pieces.

Each brownie without topping: About 206 calories, 3 g protein, 26 g carbohydrate, 11 g total fat (6 g saturated), 60 mg cholesterol, 121 mg sodium.

PRALINE-TOPPED BROWNIES: Prepare brownies as directed; cool but do not cut. In 2-quart saucepan, heat *5 tablespoons butter* and *1/3 cup packed light brown sugar* over medium-low heat until mixture has melted and bubbles, about 5 minutes. Remove from heat. With wire whisk, beat in *3 tablespoons bourbon* or *1 tablespoon vanilla extract* plus *2 tablespoons water;* stir in

2 cups confectioners' sugar until smooth. With small metal spatula, spread topping over room-temperature brownies; sprinkle *1/2 cup pecans,* toasted (see page 73) and coarsely chopped, over topping. Cut brownies lengthwise into 8 strips, then cut each strip crosswise into 8 pieces. Makes 64 brownies.

Each brownie with topping: About 297 calories, 3 g protein, 39 g carbohydrate, 15 g total fat (8 g saturated), 66 mg cholesterol, 147 mg sodium.

Blondies

These golden butterscotch favorites go from saucepan to baking pan in one easy step. For the best taste and texture, follow the instructions for determining doneness carefully. The center should still be slightly moist when the pan is removed from the oven. The blondies will firm up to just the right texture as they cool.

PREP: 10 MINUTES   BAKE: 30 MINUTES
MAKES 24 BLONDIES

1 cup all-purpose flour	1 3/4 cups packed light brown sugar
2 teaspoons baking powder	2 teaspoons vanilla extract
1 teaspoon salt	2 large eggs
6 tablespoons butter or margarine	1 1/2 cups pecans, coarsely chopped

1. Preheat oven to 350°F. Grease 13" by 9" baking pan. In small bowl, combine flour, baking powder, and salt

2. In 3-quart saucepan, melt butter over low heat. Remove from heat. With wooden spoon, stir in brown sugar and vanilla. Beat in eggs until well blended. Stir flour mixture into sugar mixture just until blended. Stir in pecans. Spread batter evenly in prepared pan.

3. Bake until toothpick inserted 2 inches from edge of pan comes out clean, about 30 minutes. Do not overbake. Blondies will firm as they cool. Cool completely in pan on wire rack.

4. When cool, cut lengthwise into 4 strips, then cut each strip crosswise into 6 pieces.

Each blondie: About 160 calories, 2 g protein, 21 g carbohydrate, 8 g total fat (2 g saturated), 25 mg cholesterol, 180 mg sodium.

Low-Fat Butterscotch Blondies

These chewy bars prove that low-fat desserts can be just as flavorful as the high-fat version. With just three grams of fat per blondie, you can have your "cake" and eat a second one too.

PREP: 15 MINUTES   BAKE: 35 MINUTES
MAKES 16 BLONDIES

1 cup all-purpose flour	3/4 cup packed dark brown sugar
1/2 teaspoon baking powder	2 large egg whites
1/4 teaspoon salt	1/3 cup dark corn syrup
3 tablespoons butter or margarine, softened	2 teaspoons vanilla extract
	2 tablespoons finely chopped pecans

1. Preheat oven to 350°F. Grease 8-inch square baking pan. In small bowl, combine flour, baking powder, and salt.

2. In large bowl, with mixer at medium speed, beat butter and brown sugar until well blended, about 2 minutes. Reduce speed to low; beat in egg whites, corn syrup, and vanilla until smooth. Beat in flour mixture just until combined. Spread batter evenly in prepared pan. Sprinkle with pecans.

3. Bake until toothpick inserted in center comes out clean and edges are lightly browned, 35 to 40 minutes. Cool completely in pan on wire rack.

4. When cool, cut into 4 strips, then cut each strip crosswise into 4 pieces.

Each blondie: About 117 calories, 1 g protein, 21 g carbohydrate, 3 g total fat (1 g saturated), 6 mg cholesterol, 94 mg sodium.

Apricot Bar Cookies

Cool the filling and the crust before assembling the layers to keep the crust from crumbling when you spread the filling over it.

PREP: 35 MINUTES PLUS COOLING   BAKE: 40 MINUTES
MAKES 40 BARS

APRICOT FILLING
1 1/2 cups dried apricots
 (12 ounces)
1 1/2 cups water
1/4 cup granulated sugar

SHORTBREAD CRUST
3/4 cup butter or margarine
 (1 1/2 sticks), softened
1/2 cup confectioners' sugar

(Shortbread Crust—continued)
1/2 teaspoon vanilla extract
2 cups all-purpose flour

STREUSEL TOPPING
1/2 cup old-fashioned or quick-cooking
 oats, uncooked
1/2 cup packed light brown sugar
1/3 cup all-purpose flour
1/4 cup butter or margarine (1/2 stick)

1. Prepare filling: In 1-quart saucepan, combine apricots and water; heat to boiling over medium heat. Reduce heat and simmer, covered, about 25 minutes, or until tender (some water will remain). With wooden spoon or potato masher, mash until smooth. Stir in granulated sugar; cool to room temperature.

2. Prepare crust: Preheat oven to 375°F. Line 13" by 9" baking pan with foil, extending foil over short ends. In large bowl, with mixer at medium speed, beat butter and confectioners' sugar until light and fluffy. Beat in vanilla. Stir in flour until well combined. With hand, pat dough firmly onto bottom of prepared pan. Bake until golden brown and set, 15 minutes. Cool to room temperature in pan on wire rack.

3. Prepare topping: In medium bowl, stir together oats, brown sugar, and flour. With fingertips, mix in butter until mixture resembles coarse crumbs.

4. Spread cooled filling over crust. Scatter topping over filling. Bake until lightly browned, 25 minutes. Cool completely in pan on wire rack.

5. When cool, lift foil with pastry out of the pan and place on cutting board; peel foil away from sides. Cut lengthwise into 5 strips, then cut each strip crosswise into 8 pieces.

Each bar: About 110 calories, 1 g protein, 17 g carbohydrate, 5 g total fat (3 g saturated), 12 mg cholesterol, 50 mg sodium.

Cherry-Cheesecake Triangles

These pretty triangles are a spectacular addition to any cookie tray. If you can't find prepared graham-cracker crumbs, it will take 12 to 13 graham crackers to make the required 1 1/2 cups. Just grind them in the food processor or put them in a plastic bag and crumble them with a rolling pin.

PREP: 20 MINUTES PLUS COOLING AND CHILLING   BAKE: 55 MINUTES
MAKES 16 TRIANGLES

GRAHAM-CRACKER CRUST
1 1/2 cups graham-cracker crumbs
6 tablespoons butter or margarine,
  melted
2 tablespoons sugar

CHEESE FILLING
1 1/2 packages (8 ounces each) light
  cream cheese (Neufchâtel), softened

(Cheese Filling—continued)
1/2 cup sugar
2 large eggs
2 teaspoons freshly grated lemon peel
1 1/2 teaspoons vanilla extract
1 cup canned cherry-pie filling

1. Preheat oven to 350°F. Grease 9-inch square baking pan. Line pan with foil, extending foil over rim; grease foil.
2. Prepare crumb crust: In bowl, with fork, stir graham-cracker crumbs, melted butter, and sugar until blended. With hand, press mixture onto bottom of prepared pan. Bake 10 minutes. Cool completely in pan on wire rack.
3. Prepare filling: In small bowl, with mixer at medium speed, beat cream cheese until smooth. Gradually beat in sugar. Beat in eggs, lemon peel, and vanilla just until blended.
4. Pour cream-cheese mixture evenly over cooled crust. Spoon dollops of cherry-pie filling over cheese mixture. With tip of knife, cut and twist through mixture to create marbled effect.
5. Bake until toothpick inserted in center comes out almost clean, about 45 minutes. Cool completely in pan on wire rack; refrigerate until ready to serve.
6. When cold, lift foil with cheesecake out of pan and place on cutting board; peel foil away from sides. Cut into 2 strips, then cut each strip crosswise into 2 squares. Cut each square diagonally into quarters.

Each triangle: About 210 calories, 4 g protein, 23 g carbohydrate, 11 g total fat (4 g saturated), 46 mg cholesterol, 220 mg sodium.

Cherry–Cheesecake Triangles

Cranberry-Cheesecake Fingers

Cranberry-Cheesecake Fingers

These rich-tasting treats have just 100 calories each! Cranberry sauce, which gives them their distinctive flavor, is available in supermarkets year-round.

PREP: 30 MINUTES PLUS COOLING AND CHILLING
BAKE: ABOUT 50 MINUTES   MAKES 48 FINGERS

GRAHAM-CRACKER CRUST
2 1/4 cups graham-cracker crumbs
1/2 cup butter or margarine (1 stick), melted
3 tablespoons sugar

CHEESE FILLING
2 packages (8 ounces each) light cream cheese (Neufchâtel), softened

(Cheese Filling—continued)
3/4 cup sugar
3 large eggs
2 teaspoons freshly grated lemon peel
2 teaspoons vanilla extract
1 can (16 ounces) whole-berry cranberry sauce

1. Preheat oven to 350°F. Grease 13" by 9" baking pan. Line pan with foil, extending foil over short ends; grease foil.
2. Prepare crust: In bowl, with fork, stir graham-cracker crumbs, melted butter, and sugar until blended. With hand, press mixture onto bottom of prepared pan. Bake 10 minutes. Cool completely in pan on wire rack.
3. Prepare filling: In small bowl, with mixer at medium speed, beat cream cheese until smooth; gradually beat in sugar. Beat in eggs, lemon peel, and vanilla just until blended.
4. Pour cream-cheese mixture evenly over cooled crust. In small bowl, mix cranberry sauce to loosen. Spoon dollops of sauce over cheese mixture. With tip of knife, cut and twist through mixture to create marbled effect.
5. Bake until toothpick inserted in center comes out almost clean, 40 to 45 minutes. Cool completely in pan on wire rack. Cover and refrigerate until firm enough to slice, at least 6 hours or overnight.
6. When cold, lift foil with cheesecake out of pan and place on cutting board; peel foil away from sides. Cut lengthwise into 4 strips, then cut each strip crosswise into 12 fingers.

Each finger: About 100 calories, 2 g protein, 11 g carbohydrate, 6 g total fat (3 g saturated), 26 mg cholesterol, 85 mg sodium.

Citrus Bars

The flavors of orange, lemon, and lime mingle beautifully in these sweet colorful bars.

PREP: 15 MINUTES PLUS COOLING   BAKE: 35 MINUTES
MAKES 36 BARS

CRUST
1 1/2 cups all-purpose flour
1/2 cup confectioners' sugar
3/4 cup cold margarine or butter
   (1 1/2 sticks)

CITRUS FILLING
1 orange
1 lemon

(Citrus Filling—continued)
1 lime
3 large eggs
1 cup granulated sugar
3 tablespoons all-purpose flour
1/2 teaspoon baking powder
1/2 teaspoon salt
1 tablespoon confectioners' sugar

1. Preheat oven to 350°F. Grease 13" by 9" baking pan. Line pan with foil, extending foil over short ends; grease foil.

2. Prepare crust: In medium bowl, combine flour and confectioners' sugar. With pastry blender or two knives used scissor-fashion, cut in margarine until mixture resembles coarse crumbs. With hand, press mixture evenly onto bottom of prepared pan. Bake until lightly browned, 20 to 22 minutes.

3. Meanwhile, prepare filling: Grate 1/2 teaspoon peel from orange, 1/2 teaspoon peel from lemon, and 1/2 teaspoon peel from lime; squeeze 2 tablespoons juice from each fruit. In large bowl, with mixer at high speed, beat eggs until thick and lemon-colored, about 2 minutes. Reduce speed to low; add citrus peel, citrus juice, granulated sugar, flour, baking powder, and salt. Beat just until blended, occasionally scraping bowl.

4. Pour citrus mixture over hot crust. Bake until filling is just set and pale golden around edges, 15 minutes. Transfer pan to wire rack.

5. Place confectioners' sugar in fine sieve and sprinkle over warm filling. Cool completely in pan on wire rack.

6. When cool, lift pastry with foil out of pan and place on cutting board; peel away foil from sides. Cut lengthwise into 3 strips, then cut each strip crosswise into 12 bars.

Each bar: About 90 calories, 1 g protein, 12 g carbohydrate, 4 g total fat (1 g saturated), 18 mg cholesterol, 90 mg sodium.

Date-and-Nut Squares

These mellow fruit-and-nut bars are easily assembled in one saucepan. Because they travel well, they are a good choice for lunch boxes.

PREP: 15 MINUTES PLUS COOLING   BAKE: 30 MINUTES
MAKES 16 SQUARES

1/2 cup butter or margarine (1 stick)   1 cup pecans (4 ounces), chopped
1 cup packed light brown sugar   1 cup pitted dates, chopped
1 1/4 cups all-purpose flour   1 large egg
1 teaspoon baking soda

1. Preheat oven to 350°F. Evenly grease 9-inch square baking pan.

2. In 3-quart saucepan, melt butter and brown sugar over medium-low heat, stirring occasionally until smooth. Remove from heat. With wooden spoon, beat in flour, baking soda, pecans, dates, and egg until well blended. Spread batter evenly in prepared pan.

3. Bake until toothpick inserted in center comes out clean, 30 to 35 minutes. Cool completely in pan on wire rack.

4. When cool, cut into 4 strips, then cut each strip crosswise into 4 pieces.

Each square: About 221 calories, 2 g protein, 30 g carbohydrate, 11 g total fat (4 g saturated), 29 mg cholesterol, 147 mg sodium.

Date Bars

A luscious brown-sugar streusel tops off moist date bars. To chop the dates easily, use scissors and dip the blades in water when they get sticky.

PREP: 40 MINUTES PLUS COOLING   BAKE: 45 MINUTES
MAKES 12 BARS

OAT CRUST AND TOPPING
1 1/4 cups all-purpose flour
1 cup old-fashioned or quick-cooking
   oats, uncooked
1/2 cup packed light brown sugar
1/2 cup butter (1 stick), softened
1/4 teaspoon baking soda
1/4 teaspoon ground cinnamon
1/4 teaspoon salt

DATE FILLING
1 container (10 ounces) pitted dates,
   chopped
3/4 cup water
2 tablespoons packed light brown
   sugar

1. Preheat oven to 375°F. Grease 9-inch square baking pan. Line pan with foil, extending foil over rim; grease foil.

2. Prepare crust and topping: In large bowl, with hand, mix flour, oats, brown sugar, butter, baking soda, cinnamon, and salt until mixture comes together. Transfer 2 cups mixture to prepared pan; reserve remaining mixture for topping. With hand, press mixture evenly onto bottom of pan. Bake 10 minutes. Cool completely in pan on wire rack. Turn off oven.

3. While crust is cooling, prepare filling: In 2-quart saucepan, cook dates, water, and brown sugar over medium heat, stirring frequently, until mixture thickens and all liquid has been absorbed, 6 to 8 minutes. Spoon date filling into bowl; cover and refrigerate until cool, about 30 minutes.

4. When filling is cool, preheat oven to 375°F. Spread filling over cooled crust; top evenly with reserved crumb mixture. Bake until topping is golden, 35 to 40 minutes. Cool completely in pan on wire rack.

5. When cool, lift pastry with foil out of pan and place on cutting board; peel away foil from sides. Cut into 4 strips, then cut each strip crosswise into 3 pieces.

Each bar: About 275 calories, 4 g protein, 47 g carbohydrate, 9 g total fat (5 g saturated), 21 mg cholesterol, 155 mg sodium.

Date Bars

Fig-and-Prune Bars

We like Calimyrna figs, the California-grown version of the Turkish Smyrna figs, in this recipe. However, you can use other dried fig varieties if you prefer.

PREP: 45 MINUTES PLUS CHILLING   BAKE: 40 MINUTES
MAKES 24 BARS

CRUST
3/4 cup unsalted butter (1 1/2 sticks), softened (do not use margarine or salted butter)
1/3 cup granulated sugar
1 large egg
2 teaspoons vanilla extract
2 cups all-purpose flour
1/4 teaspoon salt

FILLING
1 package (10 ounces) dried Calimyrna figs
1 cup pitted prunes
1 cup water
1/3 cup packed dark brown sugar
2 tablespoons fresh lemon juice

1. Prepare crust: In large bowl, with mixer at low speed, beat butter and sugar until blended. Increase speed to high; beat until light and creamy, scraping bowl occasionally with rubber spatula. Reduce speed to medium; beat in egg until blended. Beat in vanilla. With wooden spoon, stir in flour and salt until dough begins to form. With hands press dough together. Divide dough into 2 pieces, one slightly larger than the other; flatten into disks.

2. Wrap smaller disk in plastic and refrigerate. Grease 13" by 9" baking pan. Line pan with foil, extending foil over short ends; grease foil. With fingertips, press remaining dough onto bottom of prepared pan.

3. Prepare filling: With kitchen shears, cut stems from figs. In 2-quart saucepan, cook figs, prunes, water, and brown sugar over medium heat, stirring occasionally, until mixture thickens and most of liquid has been absorbed, about 10 minutes.

4. Transfer warm fig mixture to food processor with knife blade attached. Add lemon juice; process until almost smooth. Spoon fig mixture into bowl; refrigerate until cool, about 20 minutes.

5. Preheat oven to 375°F. Remove dough and filling from refrigerator. With small metal spatula, spread cooled filling evenly over dough in pan. On lightly floured surface, cut remaining dough into 20 pieces. Gently roll pieces into 1/4-inch-wide ropes (lengths will vary). Place 10 ropes diagonally across filling, about 1 inch apart; trim ends, if necessary. Repeat with remaining 10 ropes, placing them at right angles. (If ropes break, press dough together.) Bake until crust is golden, 40 minutes. Cool completely in pan on wire rack.

6. When cool, lift pastry with foil out of pan and place on cutting board; peel away foil from sides. Cut lengthwise into 4 strips, then cut each strip crosswise into 6 pieces.

Each bar: About 165 calories, 2 g protein, 26 g carbohydrate, 6 g total fat (4 g saturated), 24 mg cholesterol, 90 mg sodium.

Hermit Bars

Originating in New England in clipper ship days, these spicy fruit bars got their name from their long-keeping quality. Sailors would stow them away "like hermits" for snacking on extended voyages.

PREP: 20 MINUTES PLUS COOLING   BAKE: 13 MINUTES
MAKES 32 COOKIES

2 cups all-purpose flour	1 cup packed brown sugar
1 teaspoon ground cinnamon	1/2 cup butter or margarine (1 stick),
1/2 teaspoon baking powder	softened
1/2 teaspoon baking soda	1/3 cup dark molasses
1/2 teaspoon ground ginger	1 large egg
1/4 teaspoon ground nutmeg	1 cup dark raisins
1/4 teaspoon salt	1 cup pecans, toasted (see page 73)
1/8 teaspoon ground cloves	and coarsely chopped (optional)

1. Preheat oven to 350°F. Grease and flour two large cookie sheets.

2. In large bowl, combine flour, cinnamon, baking powder, baking soda, ginger, nutmeg, salt, and cloves.

3. In separate large bowl, with mixer at medium speed, beat brown sugar and butter until light and fluffy. Beat in molasses until well combined. Beat in egg. With mixer at low speed, beat in flour mixture just until blended, occasionally scraping bowl with rubber spatula. With spoon, stir in raisins and pecans, if using, just until combined.

4. Divide dough into quarters. With lightly floured hands, shape each quarter into 12" by 1 1/2" log. On each prepared cookie sheet, place 2 logs, leaving about 3 inches in between. Bake logs until logs flatten and edges are firm, 13 to 15 minutes, rotating cookie sheets between upper and lower oven racks halfway through baking. Cool logs 15 minutes on cookie sheets on wire racks.

5. Transfer logs to cutting board. Slice each log crosswise into 8 cookies. Transfer cookies to wire racks to cool completely.

Each cookie: About 105 calories, 1 g protein, 19 g carbohydrate, 3 g total fat (2 g saturated), 15 mg cholesterol, 80 mg sodium.

Raspberry-Walnut Streusel Bars

A beautiful and yummy cookie sandwich—two layers of buttery walnut crust filled with jewel-red raspberry jam.

PREP: 30 MINUTES   BAKE: 45 MINUTES
MAKES 24 BARS

3/4 cup butter or margarine (1 1/2 sticks), softened
1 cup sugar
1/2 teaspoon freshly grated lemon peel
1/2 teaspoon ground cinnamon
2 large egg yolks

1 teaspoon vanilla extract
2 cups all-purpose flour
1/4 teaspoon salt
1 cup walnuts (4 ounces), toasted (see page 73) and chopped
1/2 cup seedless raspberry jam

1. Preheat oven to 350°F. Evenly grease 9-inch square baking pan.

2. In large bowl, with mixer at medium speed, beat butter, sugar, lemon peel, and cinnamon until light and fluffy, occasionally scraping bowl with rubber spatula. Reduce speed to low; beat in egg yolks and vanilla until well combined, frequently scraping bowl. Add flour and salt and beat just until blended, occasionally scraping bowl. With wooden spoon, stir in walnuts (mixture will be crumbly).

3. With lightly floured hand, pat half of dough evenly onto bottom of prepared pan. Spread raspberry jam over dough, leaving 1/4-inch border all around. With lightly floured hands, pinch off 1-inch pieces of remaining dough and drop randomly on top of jam (it's okay if dough pieces touch); do not pat.

4. Bake until crust is golden, 45 to 50 minutes. Cool completely in pan on wire rack.

5. When cool, cut into 4 strips, then cut each strip crosswise into 6 pieces.

Each bar: About 176 calories, 2 g protein, 22 g carbohydrate, 10 g total fat (4 g saturated), 33 mg cholesterol, 86 mg sodium.

Whole-Wheat Fig Bars

These nutrition-packed low-fat bars make a yummy breakfast for children or adults.

PREP: 15 MINUTES   BAKE: 20 MINUTES
MAKES 12 BARS

4 ounces dried Calimyrna figs (about 3/4 cup)
1/2 cup all-purpose flour
1/2 cup whole-wheat flour
1/3 cup packed dark brown sugar
1 teaspoon ground cinnamon
1/2 teaspoon ground ginger

1/2 teaspoon baking powder
1/4 teaspoon salt
1/3 cup light (mild) molasses
2 tablespoons margarine or butter, melted
1 teaspoon vanilla extract
1 large egg white

1. Preheat oven to 350°F. Grease 8-inch square baking pan. Line pan with foil, extending foil over rim; grease foil.

2. With kitchen shears, cut stems from figs; cut figs into small pieces.

3. In large bowl, with spoon, stir figs, all-purpose flour, whole-wheat flour, brown sugar, cinnamon, ginger, baking powder, and salt until mixed. Stir in molasses, melted margarine, vanilla, and egg white just until blended and evenly moistened. With metal spatula, spread batter in prepared pan (batter will be sticky).

4. Bake until toothpick inserted in center comes out clean, 20 to 25 minutes. Cool completely in pan on wire rack.

5. When cool, lift pastry with foil out of pan and place on cutting board; peel away foil from sides. Cut into 3 strips, then cut each strip crosswise into 4 pieces.

Each bar: About 130 calories, 2 g protein, 26 g carbohydrate, 2 g total fat (0 g saturated), 0 mg cholesterol, 90 mg sodium.

Lemon Crumble Bars

To speed up the prep time of these luscious almond-topped bars, we used prepared lemon curd for the filling and made the dough in the food processor.

PREP: 25 MINUTES   BAKE: 35 MINUTES
MAKES 24 BARS

1 1/4 cups all-purpose flour
1/2 cup packed light brown sugar
1/4 teaspoon baking soda
1/2 cup cold butter or margarine
  (1 stick), cut into pieces

1/4 cup whole natural almonds,
  coarsely chopped
1/2 cup jarred lemon curd
1/2 teaspoon freshly grated lemon peel

1. Preheat oven to 350°F. In food processor, with knife blade attached, blend flour, sugar, and baking soda until mixed. Add butter and pulse just until mixture resembles coarse crumbs. Transfer 1/2 cup dough to small bowl and stir in almonds; reserve. Press remaining dough firmly onto bottom of ungreased 9-inch square baking pan.

2. In another small bowl, mix lemon curd and lemon peel; spread mixture over dough, leaving a 1/4-inch border all around. Crumble reserved dough over curd.

3. Bake until topping is browned, 35 to 40 minutes. Cool completely in pan on wire rack.

4. When cool, cut into 8 strips, then cut each strip crosswise into 3 bars.

Each bar: about 105 calories, 1 g protein, 15 g total fat (3 g saturated), 11 mg cholesterol, 60 mg sodium.

Fresh Lemon Bars

Fresh Lemon Bars

Here's an easy-to-make bar that delivers all the flavor of a lemon tart without all the extra work. They are best the day they are made, but you shouldn't have any leftovers—lemon bars are usually the first to disappear from any platter of cookies.

Prep: 15 Minutes Bake: 30 Minutes
Makes 36 Bars

1 1/2 cups plus 3 tablespoons all-purpose flour
1/2 cup plus 1 tablespoon confectioners' sugar
3/4 cup cold butter or margarine (1 1/2 sticks), cut into small pieces

2 large lemons
3 large eggs
1 cup granulated sugar
1/2 teaspoon baking powder
1/2 teaspoon salt

1. Preheat oven to 350°F. Line 13" by 9" baking pan with foil, extending foil over short ends; lightly grease foil.

2. In medium bowl, combine 1 1/2 cups flour and 1/2 cup confectioners' sugar. With pastry blender or two knives used scissor-fashion, cut in butter until mixture resembles coarse crumbs.

3. Sprinkle dough evenly into prepared pan. With floured hand, pat dough firmly onto bottom. Bake until lightly browned, 15 to 17 minutes.

4. Meanwhile, from lemons, grate 1 teaspoon rind and squeeze 1/3 cup juice. In large bowl, with mixer at high speed, beat eggs until thick and lemon-colored, about 3 minutes. Reduce speed to low; add lemon peel and juice, granulated sugar, baking powder, salt, and remaining 3 tablespoons flour. Beat until blended, scraping bowl occasionally. Pour lemon filling over warm crust.

5. Bake until filling is just set and golden around edges, about 15 minutes. Transfer pan to wire rack. Sift remaining 1 tablespoon confectioners' sugar over warm filling. Cool completely in pan on wire rack.

6. When cool, lift pastry with foil out of pan and place on cutting board; peel away foil from sides. Cut lengthwise into 3 strips, then cut each strip crosswise into 12 pieces.

Each bar: About 95 calories, 1 g protein, 12 g carbohydrate, 4 g total fat, (3 g saturated), 28 mg cholesterol, 85 mg sodium.

Hint-of-Citrus Cheesecake Bites

Perfect for entertaining, these rich, creamy squares taste even better if made a day ahead and refrigerated in the pan. Cut them just before serving. For more citrus flavor, use lemon-flavored wafer cookies instead of the vanilla.

PREP: 30 MINUTES PLUS CHILLING   BAKE: 1 HOUR 10 MINUTES
MAKES 64 CHEESECAKE BITES

CRUMB CRUST
5 tablespoons butter or margarine
3/4 teaspoon freshly grated lime peel
1 3/4 cups vanilla-wafer cookie crumbs (about 48 cookies)

CITRUS FILLING
2 large lemons
1 1/4 cups sugar
2 tablespoons cornstarch

(Citrus Filling—continued)
4 packages (8 ounces each) cream cheese, softened
1/2 cup heavy or whipping cream
5 large eggs

SOUR CREAM TOPPING
1 1/2 cups sour cream
3 tablespoons sugar
1 teaspoon freshly grated orange peel

1. Preheat oven to 350°F. Grease 13" by 9" baking pan. Line pan with foil, extending foil over short ends.
2. Prepare crust: In 10-inch skillet, melt butter over low heat; stir in lime peel. With fork, stir crumbs into melted-butter mixture until crumbs are moistened. With hand, press crumb mixture firmly onto bottom of prepared pan. Bake crust 10 minutes. Cool crust in pan on wire rack.
3. Prepare filling: From lemons, grate 1 tablespoon peel and squeeze 1/4 cup juice. In small bowl, combine sugar and cornstarch until blended. In large bowl, with mixer at medium speed, beat cream cheese, scraping bowl occasionally with rubber spatula, until smooth, about 5 minutes. Slowly beat in sugar mixture, cream, lemon juice, and lemon peel until blended, scraping bowl often. At low speed, beat in eggs just until blended (do not overbeat).
4. Pour filling over crust. Place baking pan in medium roasting pan. Place roasting pan on rack in oven. Pour enough *boiling water* into roasting pan to come halfway up sides of baking pan.

5. Bake cheesecake until toothpick inserted 1 inch from center comes out almost clean and center of cheesecake is not completely set, 55 to 60 minutes.

6. While cheesecake is baking, prepare topping: In small bowl, stir sour cream, sugar, and orange peel until blended; refrigerate until ready to use.

7. Remove cheesecake from oven. Turn off oven. Spread topping over hot cake. Return cheesecake to oven for 5 minutes (oven is off but still hot) to heat topping. Cool cheesecake completely in pan on wire rack. Cover and refrigerate at least 6 hours or overnight.

8. When cool, lift cheesecake with foil out of pan and place on cutting board; peel foil away from sides. Cut lengthwise into 8 strips; cut each strip crosswise into 8 pieces.

Each bite: About 115 calories, 2 g protein, 8 g carbohydrate, 9 g total fat (5 g saturated), 39 mg cholesterol, 75 mg sodium.

Browned-Butter Shortbread

To give the shortbread a rich, nutty flavor we used an old Scottish baking trick—we lightly browned some of the butter.

PREP: 15 MINUTES PLUS CHILLING AND COOLING   BAKE: 40 MINUTES
MAKES 16 WEDGES

3/4 cup unsalted butter (1 1/2
   sticks), slightly softened
   (do not use margarine)

1/2 cup sugar
1 3/4 cups all-purpose flour
1/2 teaspoon salt

1. In heavy 2-quart saucepan, melt 6 tablespoons butter over low heat. Cook butter, stirring occasionally, until solids at bottom of pan are a rich brown color and butter has a nutty aroma, 8 to 12 minutes. (Be careful not to overbrown butter; it will have a bitter flavor.) Pour browned butter into small bowl; refrigerate until almost firm, about 35 minutes.

2. Preheat oven to 350°F. In large bowl, with mixer at medium speed, beat sugar, cooled browned butter, and remaining 6 tablespoons softened butter until creamy.

3. With hand, mix flour and salt into butter mixture just until crumbs form. (Do not overwork dough; shortbread will be tough.) Pat shortbread crumbs onto bottom of ungreased 9-inch round tart pan with removable bottom or cake pan.

4. Bake shortbread until browned around edge, 40 to 45 minutes. Cool in pan on wire rack 10 minutes.

5. Carefully remove side of pan and transfer shortbread to cutting board. While still warm, cut shortbread into 16 wedges. Cool wedges completely on wire rack.

Each cookie: About 150 calories, 2 g protein, 17 g carbohydrate, 9 g total fat (5 g saturated), 23 mg cholesterol, 70 mg sodium.

Browned-Butter Shortbread

Brown Sugar–Pecan Shortbread

These delicious shortbread wedges make wonderful gifts. They will keep for up to a week in a tightly covered tin at room temperature and up to three months frozen.

PREP: 20 MINUTES   BAKE: 23 MINUTES
MAKES 24 WEDGES

3/4 cup butter or margarine
(1 1/2 sticks), cut into pieces
and softened
1/3 cup packed dark brown sugar

3 tablespoons granulated sugar
1 teaspoon vanilla extract
1 3/4 cups all-purpose flour
1 cup pecans, chopped

1. Preheat oven to 350°F.

2. In large bowl, with mixer at medium-low speed, beat butter, brown and granulated sugars, and vanilla until creamy. Reduce speed to low and beat in flour until blended (dough will be crumbly). With wooden spoon, stir dough until it holds together.

3. Divide dough in half. With hand, pat each dough half evenly onto bottom of two ungreased 8-inch round cake pans. Sprinkle with pecans; press lightly.

4. Bake until lightly browned around edges and firm in center, 23 to 25 minutes. Transfer pans to wire racks. With small sharp knife, cut each round into 12 wedges.

5. Cool completely in pans on wire racks.

Each wedge: About 130 calories, 1 g protein, 12 g carbohydrate, 9 g total fat (4 g saturated), 16 mg cholesterol, 60 mg sodium.

Lemon-Ginger Shortbread Triangles

For a lively twist on traditional shortbread cookies we added lemon and crystallized ginger.

PREP: 20 MINUTES   BAKE: 30 MINUTES
MAKES 48 TRIANGLES

1 lemon	1/3 cup yellow cornmeal
3/4 cup butter or margarine	1/2 cup crystallized ginger, chopped
(1 1/2 sticks), softened	1/4 teaspoon salt
3/4 cup granulated sugar	1 large egg
2 cups all-purpose flour	3/4 cup confectioners' sugar

1. Preheat oven to 350°F. Grease 13" by 9" baking pan. Line pan with foil, extending foil over short ends; grease foil.

2. From lemon, grate 1/2 teaspoon peel and squeeze 3 tablespoons juice.

3. In large bowl, with mixer at low speed, beat butter, granulated sugar, and lemon peel until blended. Increase speed to high; beat until light and fluffy, about 2 minutes. Reduce speed to low and beat in flour, cornmeal, ginger, salt, and egg just until blended (mixture will be crumbly). Sprinkle dough evenly into prepared pan. With hand, pat firmly onto bottom.

4. Bake until golden around edges and toothpick inserted in center of pan comes out clean, 30 to 35 minutes. Cool completely in pan on wire rack.

5. When shortbread is cool, in small bowl, with wire whisk or fork, mix lemon juice and confectioners' sugar until blended. Pour glaze over shortbread and, with small metal spatula, spread in even layer. Allow glaze to set, about 1 hour.

6. When glaze has set, lift foil with shortbread out of pan and place on cutting board; peel foil away from sides. Cut lengthwise into 4 strips, then cut each strip crosswise into 6 pieces. Cut each piece diagonally in half.

Each triangle: About 75 calories, 1 g protein, 11 g carbohydrate, 3 g total fat (2 g saturated), 12 mg cholesterol, 45 mg sodium.

Scottish Shortbread

To make these cookies as tender as the authentic Scottish shortbreads, which are made with softer European flours, we used silky, low-protein cake flour.

PREP: 20 MINUTES   BAKE: 40 MINUTES
MAKES 32 WEDGES

1 1/2 cups cake flour (not self-rising)   1/4 teaspoon salt
1 1/2 cups all-purpose flour   1 1/2 cups butter (3 sticks), cut into
1/2 cup sugar   pieces and softened

1. Preheat oven to 325°F. In large bowl, combine cake and all-purpose flours, sugar, and salt. Knead butter into flour mixture until well blended and mixture holds together. (Or, in food processor with knife blade attached, pulse cake and all-purpose flours and salt to blend. Add butter and pulse until mixture resembles coarse crumbs.)

2. Divide dough in half; with hand, pat onto bottom of two ungreased 8-inch round cake pans. With fork, prick dough all over to make attractive pattern.

3. Bake until golden, about 40 minutes. Remove from oven; immediately run knife around edges of pans to loosen shortbread, then cut each shortbread round into 16 wedges. Cool completely in pans on wire racks.

4. When cool, with small metal spatula, carefully remove cookies from pans.

Each cookie: About 130 calories, 1 g protein, 12 g carbohydrate, 9 g total fat (5 g saturated), 23 mg cholesterol, 105 mg sodium.

Walnut Shortbread

Just four ingredients in this easy recipe! The butter is worked into the flour mixture the traditional Scottish way—by hand.

PREP: 20 MINUTES   BAKE: 25 MINUTES
MAKES 24 COOKIES

1/2 cup walnuts, toasted (see page 73)
1 1/2 cups all-purpose flour
1/2 cup sugar
1/2 cup butter or margarine (1 stick), softened

1. Preheat oven to 325°F. In food processor with knife blade attached, process walnuts with 1/2 cup flour until nuts are finely ground.
2. In medium bowl, combine remaining 1 cup flour, sugar, and walnut mixture and stir until blended.
3. With fingertips, blend butter into walnut mixture until well combined and crumbly. With hand, press dough onto bottom of ungreased 9-inch square baking pan.
4. Bake until light golden, 25 to 30 minutes. While still warm, cut into 4 strips, then cut each strip crosswise into 6 pieces. Cool completely in pan on wire rack.
5. When cool, with small metal spatula, carefully remove cookies from pan.

Each cookie: About 94 calories, 1 g protein, 11 g carbohydrate, 5 g total fat (3 g saturated), 10 mg cholesterol, 39 mg sodium.

Chocolate Pecan Bars

If you like pecan pie, you'll love this bar. Prebaking, or "blind" baking, the crust makes for an extra crispy bar. If you don't already have pie weights, you might consider investing in one of the new pie chains. They are easy to remove from the hot crust and clean efficiently.

PREP: 25 MINUTES PLUS COOLING   BAKE: 45 MINUTES
MAKES 32 BARS

CRUST
3/4 cup butter or margarine (1 1/2 sticks), softened
1/2 cup confectioners' sugar
2 cups all-purpose flour

FILLING
2 squares (2 ounces) semisweet chocolate

(Filling—continued)
2 squares (2 ounces) unsweetened chocolate
2 tablespoons butter or margarine
2/3 cup packed light brown sugar
2/3 cup dark corn syrup
3 large eggs, lightly beaten
1 teaspoon vanilla extract
1 1/2 cups pecans, coarsely chopped

1. Preheat oven to 350°F. Line 13" by 9" baking pan with foil, extending foil over short ends.

2. Prepare crust: In medium bowl, with mixer at medium speed, beat butter and confectioners' sugar until combined. Reduce speed to low and beat in flour until combined. With lightly floured hand, press dough onto bottom and 1 inch up sides of prepared pan. Line pan with foil and fill with pie weights or dry beans.

3. Bake until lightly golden, 15 to 20 minutes. Cool to room temperature on wire racks; remove foil and weights.

4. Meanwhile, prepare filling: In 3-quart saucepan, melt semisweet and unsweetened chocolates and butter over very low heat; cool to lukewarm. With rubber spatula, stir in brown sugar and corn syrup until smooth. Stir in eggs, vanilla, and pecans. Pour filling into baked crust.

5. Bake until set, about 30 minutes. Cool completely in pan on wire rack.

6. When cool, lift pastry with foil out of pan and place on cutting board; peel away foil from sides. Cut lengthwise into 4 strips, then cut each strip crosswise into 8 pieces.

Each bar: About 175 calories, 2 g protein, 20 g carbohydrate, 10 g total fat (4 g saturated), 34 mg cholesterol, 70 mg sodium.

Flapjacks

These no-fuss brown sugar and oatmeal cookies are "quick, easy, and delicious—a perfect recipe for a young baker!" says *Good Housekeeping* Associate Research Editor Clare Ellis, who made them as a child in England.

PREP: 15 MINUTES PLUS COOLING   BAKE: 16 MINUTES
MAKES 16 COOKIES

5 tablespoons butter or margarine   **1 1/3 cup old-fashioned oats, uncooked**
1/3 cup packed light brown sugar   **pinch salt**

1. Preheat oven to 350°F. Grease 8-inch round cake pan. Line pan with foil, extending it over rim; grease foil.
2. In 2-quart saucepan, melt butter over low heat. Add sugar and cook, stirring, until well blended, 1 minute. Remove saucepan from heat; stir in oats and salt until evenly mixed.
3. Sprinkle oat mixture evenly over bottom of prepared pan; with metal spatula, firmly pat down mixture.
4. Bake until golden, 16 to 18 minutes. Let cool in pan on wire rack 10 minutes.
5. Lift foil with cookies out of pan and place on cutting board; peel foil away from sides. While still warm, cut into 16 wedges. Transfer foil with flapjacks to wire rack to cool completely.

Each cookie: About 100 calories, 2 g protein, 13 g carbohydrate, 5 g total fat (3 g saturated), 10 mg cholesterol, 50 mg sodium.

Italian Tricolors

These pretty bars, featuring the colors of the Italian flag, are found in Italian bakeries. When Food Appliances Director Sharon Franke wanted to bake her favorite cookies at home, the *Good Housekeeping* test kitchen developed this recipe especially for her.

PREP: 1 HOUR PLUS COOLING AND CHILLING   BAKE: 10 MINUTES
MAKES 36 BARS

1 tube or can (7 to 8 ounces) almond paste, broken into small pieces
3/4 cup butter or margarine (1 1/2 sticks), softened
3/4 cup sugar
1/2 teaspoon almond extract
3 large eggs
1 cup all-purpose flour

1/4 teaspoon salt
15 drops red food coloring
15 drops green food coloring
2/3 cup apricot preserves
3 squares (3 ounces) semisweet chocolate
1 teaspoon vegetable shortening

1. Preheat oven to 350°F. Grease three 8-inch square disposable or metal baking pans. Line bottom of pans with waxed paper; grease and flour waxed paper.

2. In large bowl, with mixer at medium-high speed, beat almond paste, softened butter, sugar, and almond extract until well blended (there will be some small lumps of almond paste remaining). Reduce speed to medium; beat in eggs, one at a time, until blended. Reduce speed to low; beat in flour and salt just until combined.

3. Transfer one-third of batter (about 1 rounded cup) to small bowl. Transfer half of remaining batter to another small bowl. (You should have equal amounts of batter in each bowl.) Stir red food coloring into one bowl of batter until evenly blended. Repeat with green food coloring and another bowl of batter, leaving one bowl untinted. (Batters may still have small lumps of almond paste remaining.)

4. Spoon untinted batter into one prepared pan. With metal spatula (offset, if possible), spread batter evenly (layer will be about 1/4 inch thick). Repeat with red batter in second pan. Repeat with green batter in remaining pan.

5. Bake until layers are set and toothpick inserted in center of layers comes out clean, 10 to 12 minutes, rotating pans between upper and lower oven racks halfway through baking time.

6. Cool in pans on wire racks 5 minutes. Run knife around sides of pans to loosen layers. Invert layers onto racks, leaving waxed paper attached; cool completely.

7. When layers are cool, press apricot preserves through coarse sieve into small bowl to remove any large pieces of fruit. Remove waxed paper from green layer. Invert green layer onto flat plate or small cutting board; spread with half of apricot preserves. Remove waxed paper from untinted layer; invert onto green layer. Spread with remaining apricot preserves. Remove waxed paper from red layer; invert onto untinted layer.

8. In 1-quart saucepan, heat chocolate and shortening over low heat, stirring frequently, until melted. Spread melted chocolate mixture on top of red layer (not on sides); refrigerate until chocolate is firm, at least 1 hour. If you like, after chocolate has set, cover and refrigerate stacked layers up to 3 days before cutting and serving.

9. To serve, with serrated knife, trim edges (about 1/4 inch from each side). Cut stacked layers into 6 strips. Cut each strip crosswise into 6 pieces.

Each cookie: About 125 calories, 2 g protein, 15 g carbohydrate, 7 g total fat (3 g saturated), 29 mg cholesterol, 65 mg sodium.

Honey-Granola Breakfast Bars

Sugar and spice and everything nutritious go into these yummy total breakfast bars. But don't save them just for mornings; they are a perfect high-energy treat any time of the day.

PREP: 15 MINUTES   BAKE: 30 MINUTES
MAKES 16 BARS

2 cups old-fashioned oats, uncooked   3/4 teaspoon ground cinnamon
1 cup all-purpose flour   1/2 cup vegetable oil
3/4 cup packed light brown sugar   1/2 cup honey
3/4 cup dark seedless raisins   1 large egg
1/2 cup toasted wheat germ   2 teaspoons vanilla extract
3/4 teaspoon salt

1. Preheat oven to 350°F. Grease 13" by 9" baking pan.
2. In large bowl, with wooden spoon, combine oats, flour, brown sugar, raisins, wheat germ, salt, and cinnamon until blended. Stir in oil, honey, egg, and vanilla until well combined. With wet hand, pat oat mixture evenly onto bottom of prepared pan.
3. Bake until light golden around edges, 30 to 35 minutes. Cool completely in pan on wire rack.
4. When cool, cut lengthwise into 4 strips, then cut each strip crosswise into 4 pieces.

Each bar: About 242 calories, 4 g protein, 39 g carbohydrate, 9 g total fat (1 g saturated), 13 mg cholesterol, 119 mg sodium.

Jam Crumble Bars

A food processor makes quick work of these delicious bars. For variety, spread alternating stripes of different-colored jams over the crust or drop spoonfuls of different jams and swirl them together for a marbled effect.

PREP: 15 MINUTES   BAKE: 40 MINUTES
MAKES 16 BARS

1 1/4 cups all-purpose flour
1/2 cup packed light brown sugar
1/4 teaspoon baking soda
1/4 teaspoon ground cinnamon
1/2 cup cold butter or margarine
  (1 stick), cut into 8 pieces

1/4 cup pecans, chopped
1/2 cup jam (raspberry, blackberry,
  or other fruit)

1. Preheat oven to 350°F. In food processor with knife blade attached, process flour, brown sugar, baking soda, and cinnamon until blended. Add butter and process until mixture resembles coarse crumbs and, when pressed, holds together. Transfer 1/2 cup dough to small bowl; stir in pecans. Reserve for topping.

2. Press remaining dough firmly onto bottom of ungreased 9-inch square baking pan. Spread with jam, leaving 1/2-inch border all around. With fingers, crumble reserved nut mixture over jam.

3. Bake until top and edges are browned, 40 to 45 minutes. Cool completely in pan on wire rack.

4. When cool, cut into 4 strips; then cut each strip crosswise into 4 pieces.

Each bar: About 150 calories, 1 g protein, 21 g carbohydrate, 7 g total fat (4 g saturated), 16 mg cholesterol, 85 mg sodium.

Macadamia Triangles

Macadamia Triangles

This elegant special-occasion cookie owes its fine flavor to macadamia nuts. Native to Australia, macadamia trees were planted in Hawaii near the end of the nineteenth century. The nuts are a little pricier than others, but very delicious.

PREP: 15 MINUTES PLUS COOLING   BAKE: 35 MINUTES
MAKES 32 TRIANGLES

1 cup all-purpose flour	3 tablespoons cold water
1/4 cup granulated sugar	1 jar (7 ounces) macadamia nuts
1/8 teaspoon salt	2/3 cup packed light brown sugar
6 tablespoons cold butter or	1 large egg
margarine	2 teaspoons vanilla extract

1. Preheat oven to 425°F. Grease 9-inch square baking pan. Line pan with foil, extending foil over rim; grease foil.

2. In medium bowl, combine flour, sugar, and salt. With pastry blender or two knives used scissor-fashion, cut in butter until mixture resembles coarse crumbs. Sprinkle in water, about 1 tablespoon at a time, mixing lightly with fork after each addition, until dough is just moist enough to hold together.

3. With lightly floured hand, press dough evenly onto bottom of prepared pan. With fork, prick dough in 1-inch intervals to prevent puffing and shrinking during baking. Bake crust until golden, 15 to 20 minutes (crust may crack slightly during baking). Cool completely in pan on wire rack. Turn oven control to 375°F.

4. Coarsely chop 1/2 cup macadamia nuts; reserve for topping. In food processor with knife blade attached, process remaining macadamia nuts with brown sugar until nuts are finely ground. Add egg and vanilla. Pulse until just combined.

5. Spread macadamia filling evenly over cooled crust. Sprinkle reserved chopped macadamia nuts on top. Bake until filling is set, 20 minutes. Cool completely in pan on wire rack.

6. When cool, lift pastry with foil out of pan and place on cutting board; peel away foil from sides. Cut into 4 strips, then cut each strip crosswise into 4 squares. Cut each square diagonally in half.

Each triangle: About 105 calories, 1 g protein, 10 g carbohydrate, 7 g total fat (2 g saturated), 12 mg cholesterol, 35 mg sodium.

Malted-Milk Bars

Enjoy old-fashioned soda fountain flavor in our rich, chocolate bars.

PREP: 15 MINUTES PLUS COOLING AND STANDING   BAKE: 25 MINUTES
MAKES 32 BARS

CHOCOLATE BASE
1 1/2 cups all-purpose flour
1/2 teaspoon baking powder
1/2 teaspoon salt
3/4 cup butter or margarine
  (1 1/2 sticks)
4 squares (4 ounces)
  semisweet chocolate
2 squares (2 ounces) unsweetened
  chocolate
1 1/2 cups granulated sugar
1 tablespoon vanilla extract
4 large eggs, beaten

MALTED-MILK TOPPING
3/4 cup malted-milk powder
3 tablespoons milk
1 teaspoon vanilla extract
3 tablespoons butter or margarine,
  softened
1 cup confectioners' sugar
1 1/2 cups malted-milk-ball candies
  (about 5 ounces), coarsely chopped

1. Preheat oven to 350°F. Grease 13" by 9" baking pan. Line pan with foil, extending foil over short ends; grease foil.

2. Prepare base: In small bowl, combine flour, baking powder, and salt; set aside. In heavy 3-quart saucepan, melt butter and semisweet and unsweetened chocolates over low heat, stirring frequently. Remove saucepan from heat. Stir in granulated sugar and vanilla. Beat in eggs until blended. Stir in flour mixture. Spread batter evenly in prepared pan.

3. Bake until toothpick inserted 1 inch from edge of pan comes out clean, 25 to 30 minutes. Cool in pan on wire rack.

4. Prepare topping: In small bowl, stir together malted-milk powder, milk, and vanilla until blended. Stir in butter and confectioners' sugar until blended. With small metal spatula, spread topping over cooled base; top with chopped candies. Allow topping to set, 45 to 60 minutes.

5. When topping is firm, lift pastry with foil out of pan and place on cutting board; peel foil away from sides. Cut lengthwise into 4 strips, then cut each strip crosswise into 8 pieces.

Each bar: About 200 calories, 3 g protein, 27 g carbohydrate, 10 g total fat (5 g saturated), 42 mg cholesterol, 155 mg sodium.

S'More Bars

Kids at summer camp toast the marshmallows over a campfire to make these chocolatey cookie treats. Now you can make them at home any time of the year. We included graham crackers in both batter and topping to give the recipe the flavor of the original.

PREP: 15 MINUTES   BAKE: 40 MINUTES
MAKES 24 BARS

8 graham crackers (5" by 2 1/2" each)	1 1/2 cups all-purpose flour
3/4 cup butter or margarine (1 1/2 sticks), softened	2 1/4 teaspoons baking powder
	1 teaspoon salt
1 cup packed light brown sugar	1 cup walnuts or pecans, coarsely chopped
3/4 cup granulated sugar	1 bar (7 to 8 ounces) semisweet or
1 tablespoon vanilla extract	milk chocolate, cut into small pieces
4 large eggs	2 cups mini marshmallows

1. Preheat oven to 350°F. Grease 13" by 9" baking pan. Line pan with foil, extending foil over short ends; grease and flour foil.
2. Coarsely crumble enough graham crackers to equal 1 cup pieces; set aside. With rolling pin, crush remaining graham crackers to equal 1/2 cup fine crumbs.
3. In heavy 3-quart saucepan, melt butter over low heat. Remove saucepan from heat. With spoon, stir in light brown and granulated sugars and vanilla, then stir in eggs until well blended.
4. In medium bowl, combine flour, baking powder, salt, and finely crushed graham-cracker crumbs; stir into mixture in saucepan just until blended. Stir in chopped nuts. Spread batter evenly in prepared pan.
5. Bake until top is lightly golden, 30 minutes. Remove from oven. Sprinkle with graham-cracker pieces, chocolate-bar pieces, and marshmallows. Return to oven and bake until marshmallows are puffed and golden, 10 minutes longer. Cool completely in pan on wire rack.
6. When cool, cut lengthwise into 4 strips, then cut each strip crosswise into 6 pieces.

Each bar: About 260 calories, 3 g protein, 36 g carbohydrate, 12 g total fat (2 g saturated), 36 mg cholesterol, 250 mg sodium.

Mississippi Mud Bars

Mississippi Mud Bars

These over-the-top chocolate confections freeze well and are delicious straight from the freezer as well as chilled or at room temperature.

PREP: 20 MINUTES PLUS COOLING   BAKE: 35 MINUTES
MAKES 32 BARS

MUD CAKE
3/4 cup butter or margarine (1 1/2 sticks)
1 3/4 cups granulated sugar
3/4 cup unsweetened cocoa
4 large eggs
2 teaspoons vanilla extract
1/2 teaspoon salt
1 1/2 cups all-purpose flour
1/2 cup pecans, chopped
1/2 cup flaked sweetened coconut
3 cups mini marshmallows

FUDGE TOPPING
5 tablespoons butter or margarine
1 square (1 ounce) unsweetened chocolate, chopped
1/3 cup unsweetened cocoa
1/8 teaspoon salt
1/4 cup evaporated milk (not sweetened condensed milk) or heavy or whipping cream
1 teaspoon vanilla extract
1 cup confectioners' sugar
1/2 cup pecans, coarsely broken
1/4 cup flaked sweetened coconut

1. Preheat oven to 350°F. Grease and flour 13" by 9" baking pan.
2. Prepare cake: In 3-quart saucepan, melt butter over low heat. With wire whisk, stir in granulated sugar and cocoa. Remove from heat. Beat in eggs, one at a time. Beat in vanilla and salt until well blended. With wooden spoon, stir in flour just until blended; stir in pecans and coconut. Spread batter in prepared pan (batter will be thick).
3. Bake 25 minutes. Remove from oven. Sprinkle marshmallows in even layer on top of cake. Return to oven and bake until marshmallows are puffed and golden, 10 minutes. Cool completely in pan on wire rack.
4. When cake is cool, prepare topping: In heavy 2-quart saucepan, melt butter and chocolate over low heat, stirring frequently, until smooth. With wire whisk, stir in cocoa and salt. Stir in evaporated milk and vanilla (mixture will be thick); beat in confectioners' sugar. Pour over cake.
5. Cool fudge-topped cake 20 minutes; sprinkle pecans and coconut over top. To serve, cut lengthwise into 4 strips, then cut each strip crosswise into 8 pieces.

Each bar: About 204 calories, 3 g protein, 26 g carbohydrate, 11 g total fat (5 g saturated), 44 mg cholesterol, 125 mg sodium.

Plenty-of-Peanuts Bars

Chocolate, peanuts, and peanut butter combine to make a decadently delicious bar. For an extra-special treat, cut them into twelve or sixteen rectangles and sandwich a generous scoop of vanilla ice cream between two of them.

PREP: 30 MINUTES   BAKE: 55 MINUTES
MAKES 48 BARS

1/3 cup quick-cooking oats, uncooked
1 2/3 cups all-purpose flour
1/3 cup plus 1 1/2 cups packed light brown sugar
1/2 cup margarine or butter (1 stick), softened
3 tablespoons plus 1/3 cup chunky peanut butter

3 large eggs
4 1/2 teaspoons light molasses
2 teaspoons baking powder
1/2 teaspoon salt
1 cup salted cocktail peanuts, chopped
1 package (6 ounces) semisweet chocolate chips (1 cup)
confectioners' sugar (optional)

1. Preheat oven to 350°F. Grease 13" by 9" baking pan.

2. In large bowl, with mixer at low speed, beat oats, 1 cup flour, 1/3 cup brown sugar, 4 tablespoons butter, and 3 tablespoons peanut butter until blended. Pat dough evenly onto bottom of pan and bake 15 minutes.

3. Meanwhile, in large bowl, with mixer at medium speed, beat eggs, molasses, remaining 1 1/2 cups brown sugar, remaining 1/3 cup peanut butter, and remaining 4 tablespoons butter until well combined, constantly scraping bowl with rubber spatula. Reduce speed to low; add baking powder, salt, and remaining 2/3 cup flour and beat until blended, occasionally scraping bowl. With spoon, stir in peanuts and chocolate chips. Spread mixture evenly over hot crust.

4. Bake until golden, about 40 minutes longer. Cool completely in pan on wire rack.

5. When cool, sprinkle with confectioners' sugar, if you like. Cut lengthwise into 4 strips, then cut each strip crosswise into 12 pieces.

Each bar: About 125 calories, 3 g protein, 16 g carbohydrate, 6 g total fat (1 g saturated), 13 mg cholesterol, 100 mg sodium.

Peanut Butter Rocky-Road Bars

All dressed up in toasted marshmallows, peanuts, and chocolate, these peanut butter blondies definitely have more fun. If you have trouble cutting them into bars because of the sticky marshmallow, moisten the knife blade frequently.

PREP: 15 MINUTES   BAKE: 25 MINUTES
MAKES 24 BARS

3/4 cup packed light brown sugar	1 teaspoon vanilla extract
2/3 cup creamy peanut butter	2 large eggs
1/2 cup granulated sugar	1 cup mini marshmallows
4 tablespoons margarine or butter	1/2 cup salted cocktail peanuts,
(1/2 stick), softened	chopped
1 1/4 cups all-purpose flour	1/2 cup semisweet chocolate chips
1 teaspoon baking powder	

1. Preheat oven to 350°F. Grease 13" by 9" baking pan. Line pan with foil, extending foil over short ends; grease foil.
2. In large bowl, with mixer at low speed, beat brown sugar, peanut butter, granulated sugar, and margarine until blended. Increase speed to high; beat until creamy. At low speed, beat in flour, baking powder, vanilla, and eggs until well blended, constantly scraping bowl with rubber spatula. With hand, press dough evenly onto bottom of prepared pan.
3. Bake 20 minutes. Remove from oven. Sprinkle with marshmallows, peanuts, and chocolate chips. Return to oven and bake until golden, about 5 minutes longer. Cool completely in pan on wire rack.
4. When cool, lift pastry with foil from pan and place on cutting board; peel away foil from sides. Cut lengthwise into 4 strips, then cut each strip crosswise into 6 pieces.

Each bar: About 175 calories, 4 g protein, 22 g carbohydrate, 8 g total fat (1 g saturated), 18 mg cholesterol, 100 mg sodium.

Pecan Triangles

Enjoy the rich flavor of pecan pie in a bite-size morsel. Because they keep for up to a week, these are great party make-aheads.

PREP: 30 MINUTES PLUS COOLING   BAKE: 45 MINUTES
MAKES 64 TRIANGLES

CRUST
3 cups all-purpose flour
1/4 cup granulated sugar
1/2 teaspoon baking powder
1/2 teaspoon salt
1/2 cup cold margarine or butter
  (1 stick)
1/2 cup vegetable
  shortening

FILLING
1 1/4 cups packed light brown sugar
1 cup butter or margarine (2 sticks)
3/4 cup honey
1/2 cup granulated sugar
1/4 cup heavy or whipping cream
1 pound pecans (4 cups), very
  coarsely chopped
1 tablespoon vanilla extract

1. Preheat oven to 400°F. Grease 15 1/2" by 10 1/2" inch jelly-roll pan. Line pan with foil, extending foil over rim; grease foil.

2. Prepare crust: In large bowl, combine flour, granulated sugar, baking powder, and salt . With pastry blender or two knives used scissor-fashion, cut in margarine and shortening until mixture resembles fine crumbs. With hands, firmly press crumbs onto bottom and up sides of prepared pan.

3. Bake crust until golden, 12 to 15 minutes. Remove from oven. Turn oven control to 350°F.

4. While crust is baking, prepare filling: In 3-quart saucepan, heat brown sugar, butter, honey, granulated sugar, and cream to boiling over high heat. Add pecans to sugar mixture and heat to boiling; stir in vanilla.

5. Carefully pour pecan mixture over warm crust. Bake until edges of filling begin to set (filling will be bubbly and will firm up as tart cools), 30 minutes. Cool in pan on wire rack until filling is firm to the touch.

6. When cool, invert onto rack and peel away foil. Immediately invert again onto cutting board. Cut lengthwise into 4 strips, then cut each strip crosswise into 8 pieces. Cut each piece diagonally in half.

Each triangle: About 160 calories, 1 g protein, 16 g carbohydrate, 11 g total fat (2 g saturated), 1 mg cholesterol, 80 mg sodium.

Caramel-Pecan Bars

A tasty trio of pecans, caramel, and chocolate nestled on a sweet, golden pastry crust.

PREP: ABOUT 1 HOUR PLUS COOLING AND CHILLING

BAKE: 25 MINUTES

MAKES 48 BARS

COOKIE CRUST
3/4 cup butter (1 1/2 sticks), softened (do not use margarine)
3/4 cup confectioners' sugar
1 1/2 teaspoons vanilla extract
2 1/4 cups all-purpose flour

CARAMEL-PECAN FILLING
1 cup packed brown sugar
1/2 cup honey

(Caramel-Pecan Filling—continued)
1/2 cup butter (1 stick), cut into pieces (do not use margarine)
1/3 cup granulated sugar
1/4 cup heavy or whipping cream
2 teaspoons vanilla extract
1 1/2 cups pecans, toasted (see page 73) and coarsely chopped
2 ounces semisweet chocolate, melted

1. Preheat oven to 350°F. Grease 13" by 9" baking pan. Line pan with foil, extending foil over rim; grease foil.

2. Prepare crust: In large bowl, with mixer at medium speed, beat butter, confectioners' sugar, and vanilla until creamy, about 2 minutes. At low speed, gradually beat in flour until evenly moistened (mixture will resemble fine crumbs).

3. Sprinkle crumbs in prepared pan. With hand, firmly pat crumbs evenly onto bottom of pan. Bake crust until lightly browned, 25 to 30 minutes. Place on wire rack.

4. Prepare filling: In 2-quart saucepan, heat brown sugar, honey, butter, granulated sugar, cream, and vanilla to full rolling boil over high heat, stirring frequently. Reduce heat to medium-high; set candy thermometer in place and continue cooking, without stirring, until temperature reaches 248°F or firm-ball stage (when small amount of mixture dropped into very cold water forms a firm ball that does not flatten upon removal from water).

Caramel-Pecan Bars

5. Sprinkle pecans evenly over warm crust. Pour hot caramel over nuts. Cool in pan on wire rack or until caramel is room temperature and has formed a skin on top, 1 hour.

6. With fork, drizzle melted chocolate over caramel layer. Cover and refrigerate until cold and chocolate is set, at least 1 hour.

7. When chocolate is set, lift pastry with foil out of pan and place on cutting board; peel away foil from sides. Cut lengthwise into 6 strips, then cut each strip crosswise into 8 bars.

Each bar: About 140 calories, 1 g protein, 16 g carbohydrate, 8 g total fat (4 g saturated), 15 mg cholesterol, 55 mg sodium.

TOASTING NUTS

An easy way to make your cookies taste even better is to toast the nuts, making them more flavorful.

• Preheat oven to 350°F. (If you aren't heating the oven for baking, you can use a toaster oven instead.)

• Spread out the nuts in a single layer on a rimmed baking sheet or pan; place on the middle rack in your oven.

• Heat, until lightly browned, 10 to 15 minutes, stirring occasionally so nuts in the center of the pan are moved to the edges, where they will brown faster.

• Immediately transfer nuts to a cool platter or baking pan to reduce their temperature and stop browning.*

• If you're toasting just a few nuts, heat them in a dry skillet over low heat for 3 to 5 minutes, stirring frequently.

*To remove the bitter skins from hazelnuts, toast them as directed above until any portions without skin begin to brown. Transfer the nuts to a clean, dry kitchen towel and rub them until the skins come off.

DROP COOKIES

Quick to mix up, fun to spoon onto cookie sheets, and easy to bake, drop cookies offer almost immediate gratification. No wonder drop cookies—chocolate chips in particular—are often the first cookies young bakers prepare by themselves. In this chapter you'll find all-time classics, regional specialties, international favorites, plus the latest treats—there's something here for every cookie lover.

Although drop cookies are a snap to make, you will get even better results if you bake them correctly.

• *To promote even baking,* make sure each ball of raw cookie dough is the same size. You can use a measuring spoon to scoop up equal portions of dough for each cookie or invest in a cookie scoop that will measure the dough as well as push it out onto the sheet.

• *For perfectly shaped cookies,* leave enough space between the drops of dough so that the cookies don't spread together during baking. Unless the recipe directs otherwise, 2 inches apart is a good standard.

• *To prevent the dough from spreading,* cool the sheets between batches. Spreading dough causes the cookies to run together and creates a very thin cookie that is more likely to burn. Simply run first lukewarm and then cool water over the back of the sheets between each batch.

• *To prevent cookies from sticking to the sheet,* always check greased sheets to see if they need regreasing between batches.

Almond Macaroons

We added sliced almonds to these old-fashioned favorites to make them doubly delicious. Thanks to prepared almond paste, you can whip them up in half the time it took Grandma.

PREP: 20 MINUTES   BAKE: 18 MINUTES
MAKES ABOUT 30 COOKIES

1 tube or can (7 to 8 ounces) almond paste, cut into 1-inch pieces

1/3 cup confectioners' sugar
1 large egg white
1/2 cup sliced natural almonds

1. Preheat oven to 325°F. Evenly grease and flour large cookie sheet.
2. In small bowl, with mixer at low speed, beat almond paste until crumbly. Add confectioners' sugar and egg white; beat until well blended (dough will be wet and sticky).
3. Place almonds on waxed paper. With lightly floured hands, roll dough into 1-inch balls. Roll balls in almonds, gently pressing to coat. Place balls, 1 inch apart, on prepared cookie sheet.
4. Bake until golden, 18 to 20 minutes. With wide metal spatula, transfer cookies to wire racks to cool completely.

Each cookie: About 50 calories, 1 g protein, 5 g carbohydrate, 3 g total fat (0 g saturated), 0 mg cholesterol, 3 mg sodium.

Almond Tuiles

These crisp, curved cookies—molded over a rolling pin while still hot—were named for the terra-cotta roof tiles used in the south of France. If you want to save time, you can cool them on a flat surface as you would other drop cookies—they'll taste just as delicious.

PREP: 30 MINUTES   BAKE: 5 MINUTES PER BATCH
MAKES ABOUT 30 COOKIES

3 large egg whites
3/4 cup confectioners' sugar
1/2 cup all-purpose flour
6 tablespoons butter, melted (do not use margarine)

1/4 teaspoon salt
1/4 teaspoon almond extract
2/3 cup sliced almonds

1. Preheat oven to 350°F. Grease large cookie sheet.

2. In large bowl, with wire whisk, beat egg whites, confectioners' sugar, and flour until blended and smooth. Beat in melted butter, salt, and almond extract until blended.

3. Drop 1 heaping teaspoon batter on prepared cookie sheet. With small metal spatula or back of spoon, spread in circular motion to make 3-inch round. Repeat to make 4 cookies in all, placing them 3 inches apart. (Do not place more than 4 cookies on sheet.) Sprinkle with some almonds (do not overlap).

4. Bake until golden around edges, 5 to 7 minutes. With wide metal spatula, quickly lift cookies, one at a time, and drape over rolling pin to curve cookies. When firm, transfer to wire racks to cool completely. (If you like, omit shaping and cool cookies flat.) If cookies become too firm to shape, briefly return to oven to soften.

5. Repeat with remaining batter and almonds. (Batter will become slightly thicker upon standing.)

Each cookie: About 56 calories, 1 g protein, 5 g carbohydrate, 4 g total fat (2 g saturated), 6 mg cholesterol, 48 mg sodium.

SHAPING ALMOND TUILES

Drop the Almond Tuile batter on a greased cookie sheet and spread it in a circular motion with the back of a spoon.

After baking, transfer hot cookies to a rolling pin or other cylindrical object and allow to cool in the curved shape.

Black-and-White Cookies

These giant sugar cookies with half chocolate and half vanilla frosting are popular in New York City bakeries. You can also enjoy them the way they do across the Hudson in New Jersey by just eliminating the frosting.

PREP: 20 MINUTES PLUS COOLING   BAKE: 15 MINUTES
MAKES ABOUT 12 COOKIES

2 cups all-purpose flour
1/2 teaspoon baking soda
1/4 teaspoon salt
10 tablespoons butter or margarine
  (1 1/4 sticks), softened
1 cup granulated sugar
2 large eggs

2 teaspoons vanilla extract
1/2 cup buttermilk
1 3/4 cups confectioners' sugar
2 tablespoons light corn syrup
8 to 10 teaspoons water, warmed
1/4 cup unsweetened cocoa

1. Preheat oven to 350°F. In small bowl, stir together flour, baking soda, and salt.

2. In large bowl, with mixer at medium speed, beat butter and granulated sugar until creamy. Beat in eggs and vanilla until blended. Reduce speed to low; add flour mixture alternately with buttermilk, beginning and ending with flour mixture. Beat just until combined, scraping bowl occasionally with rubber spatula.

3. Drop dough by 1/4 cups, about 3 inches apart, on two ungreased large cookie sheets. Bake until edges begin to brown and tops spring back when lightly touched with finger, 15 to 17 minutes, rotating sheets between upper and lower racks halfway through baking. With wide metal spatula, transfer cookies to wire racks to cool completely.

4. When cookies are cool, prepare white glaze: In medium bowl, mix 1 1/4 cups confectioners' sugar, 1 tablespoon corn syrup, and 5 to 6 teaspoons water, 1 teaspoon at a time, to good spreading consistency. Turn cookies over, flat side up. With small metal spatula, spread glaze over half of each cookie. Allow glaze to set 20 minutes.

5. Meanwhile, prepare chocolate glaze: In small bowl, stir together remaining 1/2 cup confectioners' sugar, the cocoa, remaining 1 tablespoon corn syrup, and remaining 3 to 4 teaspoons water, 1 teaspoon at a time, to good spreading consistency. With clean small metal spatula, spread chocolate glaze over remaining unglazed half of each cookie. Let glaze set completely, at least 1 hour.

Each cookie: About 280 calories, 3 g protein, 46 g carbohydrate, 9 g total fat (6 g saturated), 53 mg cholesterol, 190 mg sodium.

Benne Wafers

Many Southern cooks use sesame seeds in their baking, calling them by their African name, benne seeds. They originated in the Middle East and were brought to America with the slave trade.

PREP: 30 MINUTES   BAKE: 6 MINUTES PER BATCH
MAKES ABOUT 120 COOKIES

1/2 cup sesame seeds
3/4 cup all-purpose flour
1/4 teaspoon salt
1/2 cup butter (1 stick), softened
   (do not use margarine)

1 cup packed light brown sugar
1 large egg
1 teaspoon vanilla extract

1. Preheat oven to 350°F. Grease large cookie sheet.

2. Spread sesame seeds in even layer on ungreased jelly-roll pan. Bake until light golden, 10 to 12 minutes; cool on wire rack. In small bowl, stir together flour and salt.

3. In medium bowl, with mixer at medium speed, beat butter and brown sugar until combined. Reduce speed to low; beat in egg and vanilla until well blended. Beat in flour mixture and sesame seeds until combined, scraping bowl occasionally with rubber spatula.

4. Drop dough by rounded half teaspoons, 3 inches apart, on prepared cookie sheet. Bake until light brown and lacy, 6 to 7 minutes. Cool on cookie sheets on wire rack 1 minute. With wide spatula, transfer cookies to wire rack to cool completely.

5. Repeat with remaining cookie dough.

Each cookie: About 20 calories, 0 g protein, 3 g carbohydrate, 1 g total fat (1 g saturated), 4 mg cholesterol, 15 mg sodium.

Brown-Edge Wafers

The secret to perfect brown edges is to remove the cookies from the baking sheet while they're still warm and a little soft. If you allow them to cool and get crisp they may break when you lift them off.

PREP: 20 MINUTES   BAKE: 8 MINUTES PER BATCH
MAKES ABOUT 36 COOKIES

1/3 cup butter, melted (do not use
  margarine)
1/2 cup sugar
2 large egg whites

1 teaspoon vanilla extract
2/3 cup all-purpose flour
1/8 teaspoon salt

1. Preheat oven to 375°F.
2. In large bowl, with wire whisk, beat melted butter, sugar, egg whites, and vanilla until blended. Beat in flour and salt until combined.
3. Drop dough by heaping teaspoons, 2 inches apart, on ungreased large cookie sheet. Bake until edges are deep brown, 8 to 10 minutes. With wide metal spatula, quickly transfer cookies to wire rack to cool completely.
4. Repeat with remaining cookie dough.

Each cookie: About 35 calories, 0 g protein, 5 g carbohydrate, 2 g total fat (1 g saturated), 5 mg cholesterol, 30 mg sodium.

Brandy Snaps

The alcohol disappears in the oven leaving only the mellow flavor of the brandy behind, so no need to worry about giving the kids a taste. You can make the cookies flat or spiral them around the handle of a wooden spoon.

PREP: 25 MINUTES   BAKE: 5 MINUTES PER BATCH
MAKES ABOUT 24 COOKIES

1/2 cup butter (1 stick) (do not use margarine)
3 tablespoons light (mild) molasses
1/2 cup all-purpose flour
1/2 cup sugar
1 teaspoon ground ginger
1/4 teaspoon salt
2 tablespoons brandy

1. Preheat oven to 350°F. Grease large cookie sheet.

2. In 2-quart saucepan, melt butter and molasses over medium-low heat, stirring occasionally, until smooth. Remove from heat. With wooden spoon, stir in flour, sugar, ginger, and salt until blended and smooth; stir in brandy. Set saucepan in skillet of hot water to keep warm.

3. Drop 1 teaspoon batter on prepared cookie sheet; with small metal spatula or back of spoon, spread in circular motion to make 4-inch round (during baking, batter will spread and fill in any thin areas). Repeat to make 4 rounds in all, placing them 2 inches apart. (Do not place more than 4 cookies on sheet.)

4. Bake until golden brown, about 5 minutes. Cool on cookie sheet on wire rack just until edges have set, 30 to 60 seconds. Then, with wide metal spatula, quickly flip cookies over.

5. Working as quickly as possible, roll up each cookie around handle (1/2-inch diameter) of wooden spoon or dowel. If cookies become too hard to roll, briefly return to oven to soften. As each cookie is shaped, slip off spoon handle and cool completely on wire racks.

6. Repeat with remaining batter.

Each cookie: About 72 calories, 0 g protein, 8 g carbohydrate, 4 g total fat (2 g saturated), 10 mg cholesterol, 64 mg sodium.

Brandy Snaps

Brown-Sugar Drop Cookies

These easy cookies are whipped up in a saucepan instead of a bowl. The combination of brown sugar and butter gives them the flavor and aroma of butterscotch.

PREP: 30 MINUTES   BAKE: 10 MINUTES PER BATCH
MAKES ABOUT 72 COOKIES

1 1/2 cups all-purpose flour
1/2 teaspoon baking soda
1/2 teaspoon baking powder
1/4 teaspoon salt
1/8 teaspoon ground nutmeg

3/4 cup butter (1 1/2 sticks), cut
   into pieces
1 cup packed light brown sugar
2 large eggs
1 1/2 teaspoons vanilla extract

1. Preheat oven to 350°F. Grease and flour two large cookie sheets. In small bowl, stir together flour, baking soda, baking powder, salt, and nutmeg.
2. In 3-quart saucepan, heat butter and brown sugar to boiling over low heat, stirring. Remove saucepan from heat. Stir in flour mixture, eggs, and vanilla until combined. Set saucepan in skillet of warm water.
3. Drop dough by rounded teaspoons, 1 inch apart, on prepared cookie sheets. Bake until edges are browned and centers are set, 10 minutes, rotating sheets between upper and lower oven racks halfway through baking. Cool on cookie sheets on wire racks 1 minute. With wide metal spatula, transfer cookies to wire racks to cool completely.
4. Repeat with remaining cookie dough.

Each cookie: About 50 calories, 1 g protein, 6 g carbohydrate, 3 g total fat (2 g saturated), 13 mg cholesterol, 50 mg sodium.

Chewy Molasses-Spice Cookies

Dark, chewy, and warm with spices, these luscious cookies originated in Europe. Centuries ago spice cookies were made with black pepper and even mustard.

PREP: 15 MINUTES   BAKE: 13 TO 15 MINUTES PER BATCH
MAKES ABOUT 42 COOKIES

2 cups all-purpose flour
1 1/2 teaspoons baking soda
1 teaspoon ground ginger
1/2 teaspoon ground cinnamon
1/4 teaspoon salt
1/4 teaspoon finely ground black
  pepper
1/8 teaspoon ground cloves

1/8 teaspoon ground mustard
1/2 cup butter or margarine
  (1 stick), softened
3/4 cup packed dark brown sugar
1/2 cup light (mild) molasses
1 large egg
1 teaspoon vanilla extract

1. Preheat oven to 350°F. In small bowl, stir together flour, baking soda, ginger, cinnamon, salt, pepper, cloves, and mustard.

2. In large bowl, with mixer at medium speed, beat butter and brown sugar until smooth. Beat in molasses until combined. Reduce speed to low; beat in egg and vanilla until blended. Beat in flour mixture until combined, scraping bowl occasionally with rubber spatula.

3. Drop dough by rounded tablespoons, 3 inches apart, on ungreased large cookie sheet. Bake until flattened and evenly browned, 13 to 15 minutes. Cool on cookie sheet on wire rack 2 minutes. With wide metal spatula, transfer cookies to wire rack to cool completely.

4. Repeat with remaining cookie dough.

Each cookie: About 70 calories, 1 g protein, 11 g carbohydrate, 2 g total fat (1 g saturated), 11 mg cholesterol, 85 mg sodium.

Chocolate Chip Cookies

Here's America's favorite cookie. You'd better bake a double batch because they will disappear in no time. For a wonderfully decadent variation, try the White Chocolate–Macadamia Cookies below.

PREP: 15 MINUTES   BAKE: 10 MINUTES PER BATCH
MAKES ABOUT 36 COOKIES

1 1/4 cups all-purpose flour
1/2 teaspoon baking soda
1/2 teaspoon salt
1/2 cup butter or margarine (1 stick), softened
1/2 cup packed light brown sugar

1/4 cup granulated sugar
1 large egg
1 teaspoon vanilla extract
1 package (6 ounces) semisweet chocolate chips (1 cup)
1/2 cup walnuts, chopped (optional)

1. Preheat oven to 375°F. In small bowl, combine flour, baking soda, and salt.

2. In large bowl, with mixer at medium speed, beat butter and brown and granulated sugars until light and fluffy. Beat in egg and vanilla until well combined. Reduce speed to low; beat in flour mixture just until blended. With wooden spoon, stir in chocolate chips and walnuts, if using.

3. Drop dough by rounded tablespoons, 2 inches apart, on two ungreased cookie sheets. Bake until golden around edges, 10 to 12 minutes, rotating cookie sheets between upper and lower oven racks halfway through baking. With wide metal spatula, transfer cookies to wire racks to cool completely.

4. Repeat with remaining dough.

Each cookie: About 80 calories, 1 g protein, 11 g carbohydrate, 4 g total fat (2 g saturated), 13 mg cholesterol, 79 mg sodium.

White Chocolate–Macadamia Cookies: Prepare as directed but substitute *3/4 cup white baking chips* for semisweet chocolate chips and *1 cup chopped macadamia nuts (5 ounces)* for walnuts.

Each cookie: About 110 calories, 1 g protein, 11 g carbohydrate, 7 g total fat (3 g saturated), 13 mg cholesterol, 84 mg sodium.

White Chocolate–Macadamia Jumbos

Chock-full of cherries, chocolate, and macadamia nuts, just one of these cookies is a dessert by itself. But when you sandwich a scoop of your favorite ice cream between two, it's a party waiting to happen. The recipe came to us from Joanne Steinback.

PREP: 30 MINUTES PLUS COOLING   BAKE: 15 MINUTES PER BATCH
MAKES ABOUT 24 COOKIES

2 1/2 cups all-purpose flour
3/4 cup butter or margarine (1 1/2 sticks), softened
3/4 cup granulated sugar
1/2 cup packed dark brown sugar
3 tablespoons corn syrup
2 teaspoons vanilla extract
1 teaspoon baking soda

1 teaspoon salt
2 large eggs
12 squares (12 ounces) white chocolate, coarsely chopped
1 jar (6 1/2 ounces) macadamia nuts, chopped (about 1 1/3 cups)
1 1/2 cups dried tart cherries

1. Preheat oven to 325°F. In large bowl, with mixer at medium speed, beat flour, butter, granulated and brown sugars, corn syrup, vanilla, baking soda, salt, and eggs until blended, occasionally scraping bowl with rubber spatula. With spoon, stir in white chocolate, nuts, and dried cherries.

2. Drop dough by slightly rounded 1/4 cups, 3 inches apart, on ungreased large cookie sheet. Bake until lightly browned, 15 to 17 minutes. With wide metal spatula, transfer cookies to wire rack to cool.

3. Repeat with remaining dough.

Each jumbo cookie: About 310 calories, 4 g protein, 37 g carbohydrate, 16 g total fat (7 g saturated), 37 mg cholesterol, 275 mg sodium.

Chocolate-Hazelnut Macaroons

Chocolate-Hazelnut Macaroons

The fabulous combination of chocolate and toasted hazelnuts tastes even better when added to a macaroon. You can whip these up quickly and easily in the food processor.

PREP: 30 MINUTES   BAKE: 10 MINUTES PER BATCH

MAKES ABOUT 30 COOKIES

1 cup hazelnuts (filberts)
1 cup sugar
1/4 cup unsweetened cocoa
1 square (1 ounce) unsweetened
  chocolate, chopped

1/8 teaspoon salt
2 large egg whites
1 teaspoon vanilla extract

1. Preheat oven to 350°F. Toast and skin hazelnuts (see page 73). Line two large cookie sheets with foil.
2. In food processor with knife blade attached, process hazelnuts, sugar, cocoa, chocolate, and salt until nuts and chocolate are finely ground. Add egg whites and vanilla and process until blended.
3. Drop dough by rounded teaspoons, using another spoon to release batter, 2 inches apart, on prepared cookie sheets. Bake until tops feel firm when pressed lightly, 10 minutes, rotating sheets between upper and lower racks halfway through baking. Cool on cookie sheets on wire racks.
4. Repeat with remaining cookie dough.

Each cookie: About 60 calories, 1 g protein, 8 g carbohydrate, 3 g total fat (1 g saturated), 0 mg cholesterol, 15 mg sodium.

Chocolate Wows

The name says it all! Three kinds of chocolate plus pecans make a spectacular cookie.

PREP: 20 MINUTES   BAKE: 13 MINUTES PER BATCH
MAKES ABOUT 48 COOKIES

1/3 cup all-purpose flour
1/4 cup unsweetened cocoa
1 teaspoon baking powder
1/4 teaspoon salt
6 squares (6 ounces) semisweet
  chocolate, chopped
1/2 cup butter or margarine (1 stick)

2 large eggs
3/4 cup sugar
1 1/2 teaspoons vanilla extract
2 cups pecans (8 ounces), chopped
1 package (6 ounces) semisweet
  chocolate chips (1 cup)

1. Preheat oven to 325°F. Grease two large cookie sheets. In small bowl, combine flour, cocoa, baking powder, and salt.

2. In heavy 2-quart saucepan, melt chocolate and butter over low heat, stirring frequently, until smooth. Remove from heat and cool.

3. In large bowl, with mixer at medium speed, beat eggs and sugar until light and lemon colored, about 2 minutes, frequently scraping bowl with rubber spatula. Reduce speed to low. Add cooled chocolate mixture, flour mixture, and vanilla; beat just until blended. Increase speed to medium; beat 2 minutes. With wooden spoon, stir in pecans and chocolate chips.

4. Drop batter by rounded teaspoons, 2 inches apart, on prepared cookie sheets. With small metal spatula or back of spoon, spread batter into 2-inch rounds. Bake until tops are shiny and cracked, about 13 minutes, rotating cookie sheets between upper and lower oven racks halfway through baking. Cool 10 minutes on cookie sheet. With wide metal spatula, transfer cookies to wire racks to cool completely.

5. Repeat with remaining batter.

Each cookie: About 102 calories, 1 g protein, 9 g carbohydrate, 7 g total fat (3 g saturated), 14 mg cholesterol, 45 mg sodium.

Chocolate Wows

FLATTENING STIFF COOKIE DOUGH

A stiff cookie dough will bake more evenly if flattened slightly with a small metal spatula after it is dropped onto the cookie sheet.

Chocolate-Chunk Cookies

A cookie jar just isn't well-stocked unless there's something chocolate in it. This cookie is perfect for people who like a dose of decadence in their afternoon snack.

PREP: 30 MINUTES   BAKE: 10 MINUTES PER BATCH

MAKES ABOUT 36 COOKIES

2 1/2 cups all-purpose flour	1/2 cup granulated sugar
1 teaspoon baking soda	2 teaspoons vanilla extract
1/2 teaspoon salt	2 large eggs
1 cup butter or margarine (2 sticks), softened	8 ounces bittersweet chocolate, cut into 1/2-inch chunks
1 cup packed brown sugar	1 cup walnuts, coarsely chopped

1. Preheat oven to 375°F. Grease large cookie sheet.
2. In medium bowl, combine flour, baking soda, and salt.
3. In large bowl, with mixer at medium speed, beat butter and brown and granulated sugars until creamy, occasionally scraping bowl with rubber spatula. Beat in vanilla, then eggs, one at a time, beating well after each addition. At low speed, gradually add flour mixture; beat just until blended, occasionally scraping bowl. With wooden spoon, stir in chocolate and walnuts.
4. Drop cookies by heaping tablespoons, 2 inches apart, on prepared cookie sheet. Bake until lightly browned, 10 to 11 minutes. With wide metal spatula, transfer cookies to wire rack to cool.
5. Repeat with remaining dough.

Each cookie: About 170 calories, 3 g protein, 19 g carbohydrate, 10 g total fat (5 g saturated), 26 mg cholesterol, 130 mg sodium.

Coconut Cookies

To make an attractive crisscross design on these coconut-packed drop cookies simply flatten them with a fork. If the fork starts to get sticky, just dip the tines in a little flour.

PREP: 20 MINUTES   BAKE: 15 MINUTES PER BATCH
MAKES ABOUT 72 COOKIES

2 3/4 cups all-purpose flour	1 cup sugar
1 teaspoon baking powder	1 large egg
1/2 teaspoon salt	2 tablespoons milk
1 cup butter or margarine (2 sticks), softened	1 teaspoon vanilla extract
	1 1/2 cups flaked sweetened coconut

1. Preheat oven to 325°F. In medium bowl, combine flour, baking powder, and salt.

2. In large bowl, with mixer at medium speed, beat butter and sugar until light and fluffy. Beat in egg, milk, and vanilla. Reduce speed to low; beat in flour mixture just until blended. With wooden spoon, stir in coconut (dough will be crumbly). With hands, press dough together.

3. Drop dough by rounded teaspoons, 2 inches apart, on two ungreased cookie sheets. With fork, make crosshatch pattern in each cookie, flattening to 1/4-inch thickness. Bake until edges are lightly browned, 15 to 17 minutes, rotating cookie sheets between upper and lower oven racks halfway through baking. With wide metal spatula, transfer cookies to wire racks to cool completely.

4. Repeat with remaining dough.

Each cookie: About 45 calories, 0 g protein, 5 g carbohydrate, 2 g total fat (2 g saturated), 7 mg cholesterol, 41 mg sodium.

Drop Sugar Cookies

This simple old-time recipe is quick and delicious. To dress these up for a party, sprinkle them with colored sugar before baking or drizzle with melted chocolate after they come out of the oven.

PREP: 10 MINUTES   BAKE: 10 MINUTES PER BATCH
MAKES ABOUT 42 COOKIES

1 1/3 cups all-purpose flour	1 cup sugar
3/4 teaspoon baking powder	1 large egg
1/4 teaspoon salt	1 teaspoon vanilla extract
1/2 cup butter or margarine (1 stick), softened	

1. Preheat oven to 350°F. In small bowl, combine flour, baking powder, and salt.

2. In large bowl, with mixer at medium speed, beat butter and sugar until light and fluffy. Beat in egg and vanilla until blended. Reduce speed to low; beat in flour mixture just until combined, scraping bowl with rubber spatula.

3. Drop dough by heaping teaspoons, 2 inches apart, on two ungreased cookie sheets. Bake until edges are browned, 10 to 12 minutes, rotating cookie sheets between upper and lower oven racks halfway through baking. With wide metal spatula, transfer cookies to wire racks to cool completely.

4. Repeat with remaining dough.

Each cookie: About 54 calories, 1 g protein, 8 g carbohydrate, 2 g total fat (1 g saturated), 11 mg cholesterol, 46 mg sodium.

Florentines

Florentines

A pastry-shop favorite, these elegant cookies are easily made at home. The only tricky part is knowing when to remove them from the cookie sheet as they are very sticky. If you do it too soon, the cookies are too soft; if you wait until they're completely cool, they'll stick. So let them cool slightly, just until you can handle them, then move them to a rack. Always use parchment paper. Surprisingly, these ship very well: just sandwich two with the chocolate as a filling in the middle.

PREP: 40 MINUTES PLUS COOLING   BAKE: 10 MINUTES PER BATCH
MAKES ABOUT 48 COOKIES

6 tablespoons butter, cut into pieces (do not use margarine)
1/4 cup heavy or whipping cream
1 tablespoon light corn syrup
1/2 cup sugar
2 tablespoons all-purpose flour

1 cup slivered almonds, finely chopped
1/2 cup candied orange peel, finely chopped
8 squares (8 ounces) semisweet chocolate, melted

1. Preheat oven to 350°F. Line large cookie sheet with cooking parchment paper.

2. In 1-quart saucepan, combine butter, cream, corn syrup, sugar, and flour and heat to boiling over medium heat, stirring frequently. Remove saucepan from heat; stir in almonds and candied orange peel.

3. Drop batter by rounded teaspoons, 3 inches apart, on prepared cookie sheet. (Do not place more than 6 cookies on sheet.) Bake just until set, 10 minutes. Cool on cookie sheet on wire rack 1 minute. With wide metal spatula, transfer cookies to wire racks to cool. If cookies become too hard to remove, return sheet to oven briefly to soften. Repeat with remaining batter.

4. With small metal spatula or butter knife, spread flat side of each cookie with melted chocolate. Return to wire racks, chocolate side up, and let stand until chocolate has set.

Each cookie: About 70 calories, 1 g protein, 8 g carbohydrate, 5 g total fat (2 g saturated), 6 mg cholesterol, 15 mg sodium.

Lollipop Cookies

You can entertain children for quite a while by letting them decorate these fun sweets with a variety of candies. Jelly beans, gumdrops, and chocolate pieces are just some of the options.

PREP: 45 MINUTES   BAKE: 18 MINUTES PER BATCH
MAKES 12 COOKIES

1 package (18.25 ounces) favorite
  cake mix
1/2 cup butter or margarine (1 stick),
  melted
2 large eggs
12 wooden ice cream bar sticks
Vanilla Frosting (see below) or 1 can
  (16 ounces) vanilla frosting

food coloring
colored décors; assorted candies such
  as jelly beans, gumdrops, candy-
  coated chocolate pieces, nonpareils,
  black and/or red shoestring licorice

1. Preheat oven to 350°F. Grease large cookie sheet.
2. In medium bowl, with wooden spoon, stir cake mix, melted butter, and eggs until dough is blended and smooth. Drop dough by scant 1/4 cups, about 5 inches apart, onto cookie sheet to make 4 cookies (dough will be sticky). Place one end of an ice cream bar stick into each mound of dough. With hand, flatten each into a 2 1/2-inch round.
3. Bake cookies until lightly browned around edges, 18 to 20 minutes. With wide metal spatula, transfer cookies to wire racks to cool. Repeat twice with remaining dough.
4. To decorate cookies, tint frosting with food colorings as desired. Spread about 2 tablespoons frosting on each cookie. Top frosting with décors and candies.

Vanilla Frosting: In large bowl, with mixer at low speed, beat *2 1/4 cups confectioners' sugar, 6 tablespoons butter,* softened, *3 tablespoons whole milk,* and *1 1/2 teaspoons vanilla extract* until blended. Increase speed to medium-high; beat until light and fluffy, occasionally scraping bowl with rubber spatula. Makes about 1 1/2 cups.

Each frosted cookie: About 430 calories, 3 g protein, 61 g carbohydrate, 20 g total fat (8 g saturated), 58 mg cholesterol, 420 mg sodium.

Lollipop Cookies

Fruitcake Drops

An irresistible combination of coconut, chocolate, prunes, and cherries.

PREP: 30 MINUTES PLUS COOLING   BAKE: 10 MINUTES PER BATCH
MAKES ABOUT 36 COOKIES

1 3/4 cups all-purpose flour
1/2 teaspoon baking soda
1/4 teaspoon salt
1 cup packed light brown sugar
6 tablespoons margarine or butter
   (3/4 stick), softened
2 tablespoons vegetable shortening
1 large egg

1 cup pitted prunes, coarsely chopped
1 cup golden raisins
1/2 cup red candied cherries, coarsely
   chopped
1/2 cup flaked sweetened coconut
3 squares or 1 bar (3 ounces) white
   chocolate, chopped

1. Preheat oven to 375°F. Grease large cookie sheet. In large bowl, combine flour, baking soda, and salt.

2. In another large bowl, with mixer at low speed, beat brown sugar, margarine, and shortening until blended, occasionally scraping bowl with rubber spatula. Increase speed to high; beat until creamy, about 2 minutes. At low speed, beat in egg until blended. Add flour mixture, prunes, raisins, cherries, and coconut, and beat just until blended.

3. Drop dough by rounded tablespoons, about 2 inches apart, on prepared cookie sheet. Bake until edges are golden, 10 to 12 minutes (cookies will be soft). With wide metal spatula, transfer cookies to wire rack to cool. Repeat with remaining dough.

4. In heavy small saucepan, melt white chocolate over very low heat, stirring frequently, until smooth. On sheet of waxed paper, arrange cookies in single layer. Using spoon, drizzle white chocolate over cookies. Allow white chocolate to set, refrigerating if necessary.

Each cookie: About 130 calories, 1 g protein, 22 g carbohydrate, 4 g total fat (2 g saturated), 6 mg cholesterol, 70 mg sodium.

Lemony Sour-Cream Cookies

A hint of lemon adds fresh, bright flavor to sour-cream cookies. For a sparkling finishing touch, buzz some granulated sugar and a piece of lemon rind in the food processor and sprinkle it over the tops.

PREP: 15 MINUTES   BAKE: 10 MINUTES PER BATCH
MAKES ABOUT 36 COOKIES

1 cup all-purpose flour
1/4 teaspoon baking soda
1/4 teaspoon salt
6 tablespoons butter or margarine, softened

1/2 cup sugar
1/2 cup sour cream
1 teaspoon freshly grated lemon peel
1/2 teaspoon vanilla extract

1. Preheat oven to 350°F. Grease two large cookie sheets. In small bowl, combine flour, baking soda, and salt.

2. In large bowl, with mixer at medium speed, beat butter until creamy. Gradually add sugar and beat until light and fluffy. Beat in sour cream, lemon peel, and vanilla. Reduce speed to low; beat in flour mixture just until blended.

3. Drop dough by rounded teaspoons, 1 inch apart, on prepared cookie sheets. Bake until cookies are set and edges are golden, 10 to 12 minutes, rotating cookie sheets between upper and lower oven racks halfway through baking. Cool on cookie sheets on wire rack 1 minute. With wide metal spatula, transfer cookies to wire racks to cool completely.

4. Repeat with remaining dough.

Each cookie: About 49 calories, 0 g protein, 6 g carbohydrate, 3 g total fat (2 g saturated), 7 mg cholesterol, 46 mg sodium.

Moravian Spice Crisps

Our paper-thin spice crisps are a less labor-intensive version of the original. They were brought by Moravian settlers to Winston-Salem, North Carolina, in the 1700s.

PREP: 30 MINUTES   BAKE: 8 MINUTES PER BATCH
MAKES ABOUT 36 COOKIES

3/4 cup all-purpose flour
1/2 teaspoon baking powder
1/2 teaspoon ground cinnamon
1/2 teaspoon ground ginger
1/2 teaspoon ground white pepper
1/4 teaspoon ground cloves

1/4 teaspoon baking soda
1/4 teaspoon salt
1/3 cup packed light brown sugar
3 tablespoons margarine or butter, softened
1/4 cup light (mild) molasses

1. Preheat oven to 350°F. Grease large cookie sheet.

2. In large bowl, combine flour, baking powder, cinnamon, ginger, white pepper, cloves, baking soda, and salt.

3. In another large bowl, with mixer at low speed, beat brown sugar and margarine until blended. Increase speed to high; beat until creamy, about 2 minutes. At medium speed, beat in molasses until blended. With wooden spoon, stir in flour mixture.

4. Drop dough by rounded teaspoons, about 4 inches apart, on prepared cookie sheet. With finger, press each into a 2-inch round. Bake until cookies spread and darken, 8 to 10 minutes. Cool on cookie sheet on wire rack 3 minutes. With wide metal spatula, transfer cookies to wire rack to cool completely.

5. Repeat with remaining dough. Store cookies in tightly covered container.

Each cookie: About 30 calories, 0 g protein, 6 g carbohydrate, 1 g total fat (0 g saturated), 0 mg cholesterol, 45 mg sodium.

Low-Fat Oatmeal-Raisin Cookies

With their mellow brown sugar and moist raisins, these cookies taste so good no one will ever know they're low-fat. We did it by using light corn-oil spread and egg whites.

PREP: 15 MINUTES   BAKE: 10 MINUTES PER BATCH
MAKES ABOUT 48 COOKIES

2 cups all-purpose flour	1/2 cup granulated sugar
1 teaspoon baking soda	2 large egg whites
1/2 teaspoon salt	1 large egg
1/2 cup light corn-oil spread	2 teaspoons vanilla extract
(1 stick), 56% to 60% fat	1 cup quick-cooking oats, uncooked
3/4 cup packed dark brown sugar	1/2 cup dark seedless raisins

1. Preheat oven to 375°F. Grease two large cookie sheets. In medium bowl, combine flour, baking soda, and salt.

2. In large bowl, with mixer at low speed, beat corn-oil spread and brown and granulated sugars until well combined. Increase speed to high; beat until mixture is light and fluffy. Add egg whites, whole egg, and vanilla; beat until blended. With wooden spoon, stir in flour mixture, oats, and raisins until combined.

3. Drop dough by level tablespoons, 2 inches apart, on prepared cookie sheets. Bake until golden, 10 to 12 minutes, rotating cookie sheets between upper and lower oven racks halfway through baking. With wide metal spatula, transfer cookies to wire racks to cool completely.

4. Repeat with remaining dough.

Each cookie: About 67 calories, 1 g protein, 12 g carbohydrate, 2 g total fat (0 g saturated), 4 mg cholesterol, 72 mg sodium.

Oatmeal Cookies

This crunchy oatmeal cookie came to us from Darlene and Glenn Heitz of Iowa's Charles City Market. The recipe was handed down from Glenn's mother, who ground the raisins with an old-fashioned grinder.

PREP: 20 MINUTES   BAKE: 12 MINUTES PER BATCH
MAKES ABOUT 36 COOKIES

2 cups old-fashioned oats, uncooked
1 cup dark seedless or golden raisins
2 cups all-purpose flour
1 teaspoon baking soda
1/2 teaspoon salt
1 cup margarine or butter (2 sticks), softened

1 cup granulated sugar
1 cup packed light brown sugar
2 large eggs
2 teaspoons vanilla extract

1. Preheat oven to 350°F. In food processor with knife blade attached, process oats and raisins until ground; place in large bowl. Stir in flour, baking soda, and salt.

2. In separate large bowl, with mixer at low speed, beat margarine and granulated and brown sugars until blended. Increase speed to high; beat until light and creamy. At low speed, beat in eggs and vanilla, then beat in oat mixture.

3. Drop dough by rounded tablespoons, about 2 inches apart, on ungreased large cookie sheet. Bake until browned, 12 to 15 minutes. With wide metal spatula, transfer cookies to wire racks to cool.

4. Repeat with remaining dough.

Each cookie: About 165 calories, 3 g protein, 26 g carbohydrate, 6 g total fat (1 g saturated), 12 mg cholesterol, 140 mg sodium.

McIntosh-Oatmeal Cookies

Chock-full of apples, raisins, and walnuts, these big cookies bake up rich, dense, and moist, with a hint of cinnamon.

PREP: 30 MINUTES   BAKE: 20 MINUTES PER BATCH
MAKES ABOUT 24 COOKIES

1 cup margarine or butter (2 sticks),
  softened
1 1/2 cups sugar
1 1/2 cups all-purpose flour
1 teaspoon baking soda
1 teaspoon ground cinnamon
1/2 teaspoon salt
1 teaspoon vanilla extract

2 large eggs
2 medium-size McIntosh apples,
  peeled, cored, and diced (about
  2 cups)
3 cups quick-cooking oats, uncooked
1 cup dark seedless raisins
3/4 cup walnuts, chopped

1. Preheat oven to 350°F.

2. In large bowl, with mixer at medium speed, beat margarine and sugar until light and fluffy, about 5 minutes. Add flour, baking soda, cinnamon, salt, vanilla, and eggs; beat just until blended, occasionally scraping bowl with rubber spatula. With wooden spoon, stir in apples, oats, raisins, and walnuts.

3. Drop dough by level 1/4 cups, about 3 inches apart, on two ungreased large cookie sheets. Bake until golden, 20 to 25 minutes, rotating cookie sheets between upper and lower oven racks halfway through baking time. With wide metal spatula, transfer cookies to wire racks to cool completely.

4. Repeat with remaining dough.

Each cookie: About 275 calories, 5 g protein, 39 g carbohydrate, 12 g total fat (2 g saturated), 18 mg cholesterol, 205 mg sodium.

Grandmother's Oatmeal-Raisin Cookies

Grandmother's Oatmeal-Raisin Cookies

These family favorites bake up crisp and golden. If you prefer softer oatmeal cookies, reduce the baking time by about two minutes, and store them in a tight container with a slice of fresh bread or apple. Replace the bread or apple every other day.

PREP: 15 MINUTES   BAKE: 15 MINUTES PER BATCH
MAKES ABOUT 24 COOKIES

3/4 cup all-purpose flour
1/2 teaspoon baking soda
1/4 teaspoon salt
1/2 cup butter or margarine (1 stick), softened
1/2 cup granulated sugar
1/3 cup packed light brown sugar

1 large egg
2 teaspoons vanilla extract
1 1/2 cups old-fashioned or quick-cooking oats, uncooked
3/4 cup dark seedless raisins or chopped pitted prunes

1. Preheat oven to 350°F. In small bowl, combine flour, baking soda, and salt.

2. In large bowl, with mixer at medium speed, beat butter and granulated and brown sugars until light and fluffy. Beat in egg and vanilla until blended. Reduce speed to low; beat in flour mixture just until blended. With wooden spoon, stir in oats and raisins.

3. Drop dough by heaping tablespoons, 2 inches apart, on two ungreased large cookie sheets. Bake until golden, about 15 minutes, rotating cookie sheets between upper and lower oven racks halfway through baking. With wide metal spatula, transfer cookies to wire racks to cool completely.

4. Repeat with remaining dough.

Each cookie: About 113 calories, 2 g protein, 17 g carbohydrate, 4 g total fat (2 g saturated), 19 mg cholesterol, 94 mg sodium.

Chewy Peanut Butter Cookies

These cookies work best with supermarket brands of peanut butter. The crosshatch pattern is traditional on peanut butter cookies, but you'll get no complaints if the tops are flattened with a spatula or spoon.

PREP: 35 MINUTES PLUS CHILLING   BAKE: 12 MINUTES PER BATCH
MAKES ABOUT 60 COOKIES

2 3/4 cups all-purpose flour	1 cup creamy peanut butter
1 teaspoon baking powder	1 cup packed brown sugar
1/2 teaspoon baking soda	1/2 cup granulated sugar
1/4 teaspoon salt	2 tablespoons dark corn syrup
1 cup butter or margarine (2 sticks), softened	2 teaspoons vanilla extract
	2 large eggs

1. Preheat oven to 375°F. In medium bowl, combine flour, baking powder, baking soda, and salt.

2. In large bowl, with mixer at medium speed, beat butter, peanut butter, and brown and granulated sugars until creamy, occasionally scraping bowl with rubber spatula. Beat in corn syrup, vanilla, then eggs, one at a time, beating well after each addition. At low speed, gradually add flour mixture; beat just until blended, occasionally scraping bowl. Cover and refrigerate dough 30 minutes for easier shaping.

3. Shape dough by rounded tablespoons into 1 1/2-inch balls. Place balls, 2 inches apart, on ungreased large cookie sheet. With floured tines of fork, press and flatten each ball, making a crisscross pattern. Bake until pale golden, 12 to 13 minutes. With wide metal spatula, transfer cookies to wire rack to cool.

4. Repeat with remaining dough.

Each cookie: About 100 calories, 2 g protein, 11 g carbohydrate, 6 g total fat (3 g saturated), 16 mg cholesterol, 85 mg sodium.

Making Crosshatch Marks

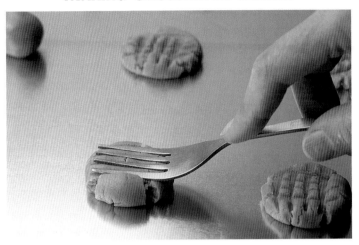

Whether you drop the dough or shape it into balls, flattening the peanut butter dough with a fork gives it its classic finish.

Rich Chocolate-Cherry Cookies

We received this luscious recipe from Lori Conforti, who got it from her mother-in-law. Now Lori's children are growing up with them, just as her husband did.

PREP: 30 MINUTES   BAKE: 13 MINUTES PER BATCH
MAKES ABOUT 36 COOKIES

8 squares (8 ounces) semisweet
  chocolate, coarsely chopped
6 tablespoons margarine or butter,
  cut into pieces
3/4 cup sugar
2 teaspoons vanilla extract
2 large eggs

1/4 cup all-purpose flour
1/4 cup unsweetened cocoa
1/2 teaspoon baking powder
1/4 teaspoon salt
1 package (6 ounces) semisweet
  chocolate chips (1 cup)
1 cup dried tart cherries

1. Preheat oven to 350°F. In 3-quart saucepan, melt chocolate and margarine over low heat, stirring frequently. Remove saucepan from heat. With wire whisk, stir in sugar and vanilla until blended. Whisk in eggs, one at a time. With wooden spoon, stir in flour, cocoa, baking powder, and salt. Add chocolate chips and cherries; stir just until evenly mixed.

2. Drop dough by rounded tablespoons, 1 1/2 inches apart, on ungreased large cookie sheet. Bake until tops of cookies are set, 13 to 15 minutes. Cool on cookie sheet on wire rack 1 minute. With wide metal spatula, transfer cookies to wire rack to cool completely.

3. Repeat with remaining dough.

Each cookie: About 105 calories, 1 g protein, 16 g carbohydrate, 5 g total fat (1 g saturated), 12 mg cholesterol, 55 mg sodium.

Ricotta-Cheese Cookies

These soft, Italian-style cookies came to us from Naoma R. Felt of Bradenton, Florida. They are easy to make and freeze well, so why not bake several batches and stock the freezer.

PREP: 30 MINUTES PLUS COOLING   BAKE: 15 MINUTES PER BATCH
MAKES ABOUT 72 COOKIES

1 cup margarine or butter (2 sticks), softened
2 cups granulated sugar
1 container (15 ounces) ricotta cheese
2 teaspoons vanilla extract
2 large eggs

4 cups all-purpose flour
2 tablespoons baking powder
1 teaspoon salt
1 1/2 cups confectioners' sugar
3 tablespoons milk
colored sugar crystals

1. Preheat oven to 350°F. In large bowl, with mixer at low speed, beat margarine and granulated sugar until blended. Increase speed to high; beat until light and fluffy, about 5 minutes. At medium speed, beat in ricotta, vanilla, and eggs until well combined. Reduce speed to low. Add flour, baking powder, and salt; beat until dough forms.

2. Drop dough by level tablespoons, about 2 inches apart, on ungreased large cookie sheet. Bake until cookies are very lightly golden, about 15 minutes (they will be soft). With wide metal spatula, transfer cookies to wire rack to cool. Repeat with remaining dough.

3. When cookies are cool, prepare icing: In small bowl, stir confectioners' sugar and milk until smooth. With small metal spatula or knife, spread icing on cookies; sprinkle with colored sugar crystals. Set aside on wire rack until icing is completely dry, about 1 hour.

Each cookie: About 90 calories, 1 g protein, 14 g carbohydrate, 3 g total fat (1 g saturated), 3 mg cholesterol, 100 mg sodium.

Soft Applesauce-Raisin Cookies

A Granny Smith apple adds moisture and texture, while the lemon glaze gives an appealing shine to these old-fashioned beauties.

PREP: 35 MINUTES   BAKE: 20 MINUTES

MAKES ABOUT 45 COOKIES

APPLESAUCE-RAISIN COOKIES
2 cups all-purpose flour
1/2 teaspoon baking powder
1/2 teaspoon baking soda
1/2 teaspoon ground cinnamon
1/4 teaspoon ground allspice
1/4 teaspoon salt
1/2 cup butter or margarine (1 stick), softened
1/2 cup granulated sugar
1/4 cup packed brown sugar
1 large egg

(Applesauce-Raisin Cookies—continued)
1 cup unsweetened applesauce
1 teaspoon vanilla extract
1 medium Granny Smith apple, peeled, cored, and diced
1 cup dark raisins
1 cup walnuts, coarsely chopped (optional)

LEMON GLAZE
1 cup confectioners' sugar
2 tablespoons fresh lemon juice

1. Preheat oven to 375°F. Grease two large cookie sheets.

2. Prepare cookies: In medium bowl, combine flour, baking powder, baking soda, cinnamon, allspice, and salt.

3. In large bowl, with mixer at medium speed, beat butter and granulated and brown sugars until light and fluffy. Reduce speed to low; beat in egg, applesauce, and vanilla until well combined. Beat in flour mixture until blended. With wooden spoon, stir in apple, raisins, and walnuts, if using.

4. Drop dough by rounded tablespoons, 1 inch apart, on prepared cookie sheets. Bake until lightly browned around edges and set, 20 to 22 minutes, rotating cookie sheets between upper and lower oven racks halfway through baking.

5. While cookies bake, prepare glaze: In small bowl, stir confectioners' sugar and lemon juice until smooth.

6. With wide metal spatula, transfer cookies to wire racks. With pastry brush, brush glaze over warm cookies; cool completely.

Each cookie: About 80 calories, 1 g protein, 14 g carbohydrate, 2 g total fat (1 g saturated), 11 mg cholesterol, 55 mg sodium.

Sour-Cream Cookies

Subtle nutmeg flavor and a light cakelike texture make these an elegant partner for a cup of afternoon tea.

PREP: 25 MINUTES BAKE: 10 MINUTES PER BATCH
MAKES ABOUT 30 COOKIES

1 3/4 cups all-purpose flour
1 teaspoon baking powder
1/2 teaspoon salt
1/4 teaspoon baking soda
1/4 teaspoon ground nutmeg
1/2 cup butter or margarine (1 stick), softened

1 cup plus 2 tablespoons granulated sugar
1 large egg
2 teaspoons vanilla extract
1/2 cup sour cream

1. Preheat oven to 400°F. Grease large cookie sheet.

2. In medium bowl, combine flour, baking powder, salt, baking soda, and nutmeg.

3. In large bowl, with mixer at medium speed, beat butter and 1 cup sugar until creamy, occasionally scraping bowl with rubber spatula. Beat in egg and vanilla, then sour cream, until well combined. With mixer at low speed, beat in flour mixture just until blended, occasionally scraping bowl.

4. Drop dough by rounded tablespoons, 2 inches apart, on prepared cookie sheet. Sprinkle lightly with some of remaining sugar. Bake until edges are lightly browned, 10 to 12 minutes. With wide metal spatula, transfer cookies to wire rack to cool.

5. Repeat with remaining dough and sugar.

Each cookie: About 95 calories, 1 g protein, 13 g carbohydrate, 4 g total fat (3 g saturated), 17 mg cholesterol, 100 mg sodium.

Toffee–Peanut Butter Rounds

Alice Garbarini Hurley brought us this recipe, which makes a delicious and welcome gift any time of the year. You can bake them up yourself or simply layer all the dry ingredients in a 1 1/2-quart jar with a tight-fitting lid, tie it with ribbon, and attach the recipe. The dry ingredients can be stored at room temperature for up to three months.

PREP: 30 MINUTES   BAKE: 10 MINUTES PER BATCH
MAKES ABOUT 54 COOKIES

1 cup butter or margarine (2 sticks), melted and cooled
2 large eggs
2 1/4 cups all-purpose flour
1 cup peanut butter chips
4 chocolate-covered toffee candy bars (1.4 ounces each), coarsely chopped (about 1 cup)

3/4 cup old-fashioned oats, uncooked
1/2 cup granulated sugar
1/2 cup packed light brown sugar
1/2 cup packed dark brown sugar
1/2 teaspoon baking soda
1/2 teaspoon salt

1. Preheat oven to 375°F. In large bowl, with mixer at medium speed, beat butter and eggs until blended. Add flour, peanut butter chips, chopped candy bars, oats, granulated and brown sugars, baking soda, and salt; beat until well mixed, occasionally scraping bowl with rubber spatula.
2. Drop dough by rounded tablespoons, 2 inches apart, on ungreased large cookie sheet. Bake until lightly browned, 10 minutes. With wide metal spatula, transfer cookies to wire rack to cool.
3. Repeat with remaining dough.

Each cookie: About 125 calories, 2 g protein, 15 g carbohydrate, 6 g total fat (4 g saturated), 19 mg cholesterol, 90 mg sodium.

Triple-Chocolate Chubbies

We added more chocolate, walnuts, and pecans to a dense brownie-like batter to create a big, fat cookie that became an instant tradition in our test kitchen.

PREP: 25 MINUTES PLUS COOLING   BAKE: 14 MINUTES PER BATCH
MAKES ABOUT 24 COOKIES

1/4 cup all-purpose flour	1 cup sugar
1/4 cup unsweetened cocoa	2 teaspoons vanilla extract
1/2 teaspoon baking powder	2 large eggs
1/4 teaspoon salt	1 package (6 ounces) semisweet
8 squares (8 ounces) semisweet	chocolate chips (1 cup)
chocolate, chopped	1/2 cup pecans, chopped
6 tablespoons butter or margarine,	1/2 cup walnuts, chopped
cut into pieces	

1. Preheat oven to 350°F. In small bowl, stir together flour, cocoa, baking powder, and salt.

2. In 3-quart saucepan, melt chopped chocolate and butter over low heat, stirring frequently, until smooth. Pour into large bowl; cool to lukewarm. Stir in sugar and vanilla until blended. Stir in eggs, one at a time, until well blended. Add flour mixture and stir until combined (batter will be thin). Stir in chocolate chips, pecans, and walnuts.

3. Drop batter by heaping tablespoons, 1 1/2 inches apart, on ungreased large cookie sheet. Bake until set, 14 minutes. Cool on cookie sheet on wire rack 2 minutes. With wide metal spatula, carefully transfer cookies to wire rack to cool completely.

4. Repeat with remaining batter.

Each cookie: About 180 calories, 2 g protein, 21 g carbohydrate, 11 g total fat (5 g saturated), 26 mg cholesterol, 70 mg sodium.

Whoopie Pies

We discovered these soft, marshmallow-filled, chocolate sandwiches at a farmer's market and just loved them. So we re-created the recipe and now you can bake them at home.

PREP: 30 MINUTES PLUS COOLING BAKE: 12 MINUTES
MAKES 12 WHOOPIE PIES

COOKIES
2 cups all-purpose flour
1 cup granulated sugar
1/2 cup unsweetened cocoa
1 teaspoon baking soda
6 tablespoons butter or margarine,
  melted
3/4 cup milk
1 large egg
1 teaspoon vanilla extract
1/4 teaspoon salt

MARSHMALLOW-CREME FILLING
6 tablespoons butter or margarine,
  slightly softened
1 cup confectioners' sugar
1 jar (7 to 7 1/2 ounces) marshmallow
  creme
1 teaspoon vanilla extract

1. Preheat oven to 350°F. Grease two large cookie sheets.

2. Prepare cookies: In large bowl, combine flour, granulated sugar, cocoa, and baking soda. Stir in melted butter, milk, egg, vanilla, and salt until smooth.

3. Drop dough by heaping tablespoons, 2 inches apart, on prepared cookie sheets. (There will be 12 rounds per sheet.) Bake until puffy and toothpick inserted in center comes out clean, 12 to 14 minutes, rotating sheets between upper and lower racks halfway through baking. With wide metal spatula, transfer cookies to wire racks to cool completely.

4. When cookies are cool, prepare filling: In large bowl, with mixer at medium speed, beat softened butter until smooth. Reduce speed to low; gradually beat in confectioners' sugar. Beat in marshmallow creme and vanilla until smooth.

5. Spread 1 rounded tablespoon filling on flat side of 12 cookies. Top with remaining cookies.

Each whoopie pie: About 365 calories, 4 g protein, 59 g carbohydrate, 14 g total fat (8 g saturated), 51 mg cholesterol, 290 mg sodium.

Whoopie Pies

ROLLED COOKIES

Here are the cookies dreams are made of. Rolled cookies might require a bit more time and effort to prepare, but the pretty cutouts or traditional roll-ups that result are a gift of love, works of art to be appreciated visually before savoring.

However that doesn't mean they are just for special occasions. Mixing, rolling, and cutting rolled cookies make a perfect rainy-weekend activity to enjoy with your family. Most rolled-cookie doughs are very easy to make, and you can have fun cutting them into all sorts of shapes using cookie cutters or into rectangles with a pastry wheel.

They are great make-aheads, too. You can prepare several batches at once and keep the dough in the freezer for up to three months, all ready to roll out and bake. For even quicker baking and less cleanup, you can roll out the dough between sheets of waxed paper and tightly wrap it before freezing. Then, when you want cookies, all you have to do is cut the sheets of dough into shapes.

Here are some tips that will make it easy.

• *Chill the dough before rolling.* A few rolled-cookie doughs are stiff enough to roll out shortly after they are prepared, but most require several hours of chilling. For convenience, you might want to make the dough a day ahead and refrigerate overnight.

• *For easier rolling,* dust the work surface lightly and evenly with flour before you roll out the dough. Also rub the rolling pin with flour to keep it from sticking to the dough.

• *For easier cleanup,* you can roll out dough between sheets of waxed paper. Flour both the waxed paper and your rolling pin.

• *Roll out one portion of chilled dough at a time* and keep the remaining dough well wrapped in the refrigerator. It's difficult to roll warm, sticky dough.

• *If chilled dough cracks* when rolled, let it stand at room temperature to soften slightly, then try again.

• *Cut out cookies as close together* as possible so that you have less dough to reroll.

Biscochitos

These flaky, rich Mexican cookies are traditionally made with lard.
We substituted half butter and half shortening, with delicious results.

PREP: 18 MINUTES   BAKE: 11 MINUTES PER BATCH
MAKES ABOUT 76 COOKIES

3 cups all-purpose flour
1 1/2 teaspoons baking powder
1/4 teaspoon salt
1/2 cup butter or margarine (1 stick), softened
1/2 cup vegetable shortening

1 cup sugar
2 teaspoons anise seeds
1 large egg yolk
1/4 cup sherry or sweet wine
4 teaspoons ground cinnamon

1. Preheat oven to 375°F. In large bowl, stir together flour, baking powder, and salt.
2. In separate large bowl, with mixer at medium speed, beat butter, shortening, and 1/2 cup sugar until light and fluffy. Beat in anise seeds and egg yolk until well combined. Beat in sherry until smooth. Reduce speed to low and beat in flour mixture until well combined.
3. Divide dough into 4 equal pieces. On lightly floured surface, roll out one piece of dough, 1/4 inch thick.
4. In small bowl, stir together remaining 1/2 cup sugar and cinnamon. Sprinkle one-fourth of cinnamon-sugar mixture over dough. With 2-inch decorative cookie cutter, cut out as many cookies as possible. (Cut cookies as close to each other as possible; do not reroll scraps).
5. Place cookies, 1 inch apart, on two ungreased large cookie sheets. Bake until set, 11 minutes, rotating sheets between upper and lower racks halfway through baking. Cool on cookie sheets on wire racks 1 minute. With wide metal spatula, transfer to wire racks to cool completely.
6. Repeat with remaining dough and cinnamon-sugar.

Each cookie: About 50 calories, 1 g protein, 6 g carbohydrate, 3 g total fat (1 g saturated), 6 mg cholesterol, 30 mg sodium.

Brown Sugar Cut-Out Cookies

This cookie is especially easy to roll and cut out because the buttery dough is made with brown sugar. You can give the cookies a quick sprinkle with granulated sugar before baking or frost and decorate them after they have baked and cooled.

PREP: 35 MINUTES PLUS CHILLING   BAKE: 10 MINUTES PER BATCH
MAKES ABOUT 76 COOKIES

2 cups all-purpose flour
1/2 teaspoon baking soda
1/4 teaspoon salt
1/2 cup butter or margarine (1 stick), softened

3/4 cup packed light brown sugar
1 large egg
1/4 cup granulated sugar or
   Ornamental Frosting (see page 248)

1. Preheat oven to 350°F. In medium bowl, stir together flour, baking soda, and salt.

2. In large bowl, with mixer at medium speed, beat butter and brown sugar until combined. Reduce speed to low and beat in egg until blended. Beat in flour mixture until combined, scraping bowl occasionally with rubber spatula.

3. Shape dough into 2 balls; flatten each slightly. Wrap 1 ball in waxed paper and refrigerate while working with remaining half.

4. On lightly floured surface, with floured rolling pin, roll 1 ball of dough 1/8 inch thick. With floured 2-inch cookie cutters, cut out as many cookies as possible; reserve trimmings. Place cookies, about 1/2 inch apart, on ungreased large cookie sheet.

5. Sprinkle granulated sugar over cookies, if desired, or bake without sugar and frost when cool. Bake until edges begin to brown, 10 minutes. With wide metal spatula, transfer cookies to wire rack to cool completely.

6. Repeat with remaining dough, trimmings, and granulated sugar, if using.

Each cookie: About 35 calories, 0 g protein, 5 g carbohydrate, 1 g total fat (1 g saturated), 6 mg cholesterol, 30 mg sodium.

Butterscotch Fingers

When butter and brown sugar are combined, there's an almost magical transformation to the flavor we know as butterscotch. Here, pecans accentuate the richness.

PREP: 30 MINUTES PLUS CHILLING   BAKE: 12 MINUTES PER BATCH
MAKES ABOUT 96 COOKIES

2 1/3 cups all-purpose flour
1/2 teaspoon baking powder   1 cup packed dark brown sugar
1/2 teaspoon salt   1 teaspoon vanilla extract
1 cup butter or margarine (2 sticks),   1 large egg
  softened   3/4 cup pecans, chopped

1. In medium bowl, combine flour, baking powder, and salt.
2. In large bowl, with mixer at medium speed, beat butter and sugar until creamy, occasionally scraping bowl with rubber spatula. Beat in vanilla, then egg. At low speed, gradually add flour mixture; beat just until blended, occasionally scraping bowl. With wooden spoon, stir in pecans.
3. Shape dough into a 12" by 3 3/4" by 1" brick. Wrap brick in plastic and refrigerate until firm enough to slice, at least 6 hours or overnight. Or place brick in freezer for about 2 hours. (If using margarine, freeze brick overnight.)
4. Preheat oven to 350°F. Grease large cookie sheet. With sharp knife, cut brick crosswise into 1/8-inch-thick slices. Place slices, 1 inch apart, on prepared cookie sheet. Bake until lightly browned around edges, 12 to 14 minutes. With wide metal spatula, transfer cookies to wire rack to cool.
5. Repeat with remaining dough.

Each cookie: About 45 calories, 1 g protein, 5 g carbohydrate, 3 g total fat (1 g saturated), 8 mg cholesterol, 38 mg sodium.

Cinnamon Twists

Good Housekeeping reader Carrie Deegan of Glen Cove, New York, sent us this recipe for tender cream-cheese cookies coated with walnut-and-cinnamon sugar. She created the recipe for her homemade-cookie business.

PREP: 1 HOUR PLUS CHILLING   BAKE: 15 MINUTES PER BATCH
MAKES 66 COOKIES

1 package (8 ounces) cream cheese,   3/4 cup walnuts
  softened   1 cup sugar
1 cup margarine or butter (2 sticks), 2 teaspoons ground cinnamon
  softened   1 large egg, beaten
2 1/2 cups all-purpose flour

1. In large bowl, with mixer at low speed, beat cream cheese and margarine until blended, constantly scraping bowl with rubber spatula. Increase speed to high; beat until light and creamy, about 2 minutes. With mixer at low speed, gradually add 1 cup flour and beat until blended. With wooden spoon, stir in remaining 1 1/2 cups flour until smooth.

2. On lightly floured sheet of plastic wrap, pat dough into 9-inch square. Wrap in the plastic and refrigerate until dough is firm enough to roll, 2 hours.

3. Meanwhile, in food processor with knife blade attached, process walnuts and 1/4 cup sugar until walnuts are finely ground. In small bowl, stir cinnamon, remaining 3/4 cup sugar, and walnut mixture until well blended; set aside.

4. Preheat oven to 400°F. Grease large cookie sheet. On lightly floured sheet of waxed paper, with floured rolling pin, roll dough square into 11" by 10 1/2" rectangle. With pastry brush, brush some beaten egg over top of dough rectangle. Sprinkle with half of walnut mixture; gently press walnut mixture into dough. Invert dough rectangle onto another sheet of lightly floured waxed paper, nut side down. Brush with beaten egg, sprinkle with remaining walnut mixture, and gently press nut mixture into dough.

5. Cut dough lengthwise into three 3 1/2-inch-wide bars, then cut each bar crosswise into 1/2-inch-wide strips to make sixty-six 3 1/2" by 1/2" strips in all. Twist each strip twice, then place, about 1 inch apart, on prepared cookie sheet.

6. Bake twists until lightly browned, 15 to 17 minutes. With wide metal spatula, gently loosen twists from cookie sheet and transfer to wire rack to cool.

7. Repeat with remaining strips.

Each cookie: About 75 calories, 1 g protein, 7 g carbohydrate, 5 g total fat (1 g saturated), 7 mg cholesterol, 50 mg sodium.

Classic Sugar Cookies

Here's the perfect, all-purpose sugar cookie dough. You can slice it into diamonds with a knife and sprinkle with colored sugar or cut it into shapes with cookie cutters and decorate with frosting. For a pretty dessert, press dough into tart shape, bake, then fill with berries and cream.

PREP: 1 HOUR 30 MINUTES PLUS CHILLING
BAKE: 12 MINUTES PER BATCH
MAKES ABOUT 76 COOKIES

3 cups all-purpose flour
1/2 teaspoon baking powder
1/2 teaspoon salt
1 cup butter (2 sticks), softened
   (do not use margarine)

1 1/2 cups sugar
2 large eggs
1 teaspoon vanilla extract

1. In large bowl, combine flour, baking powder, and salt. In separate large bowl, with mixer at low speed, beat butter and sugar until blended. Increase speed to high; beat until light and fluffy, about 5 minutes. Reduce speed to low; beat in eggs and vanilla until mixed, then beat in flour mixture just until blended, occasionally scraping bowl with rubber spatula. Divide dough into 4 equal pieces; flatten each into a disk. Wrap each disk in plastic and refrigerate overnight.

2. Preheat oven to 350°F. On lightly floured surface, with floured rolling pin, roll 1 piece of dough until slightly less than 1/4 inch thick; keep remaining dough refrigerated. With floured 3- to 4-inch cookie cutters, cut dough into as many cookies as possible; reserve trimmings. Place cookies, 1 inch apart, on two ungreased large cookie sheets.

3. Bake until edges are golden, 12 to 15 minutes, rotating cookie sheets between upper and lower oven racks halfway through baking. With wide metal spatula, transfer cookies to wire racks to cool completely.

4. Repeat with remaining dough and trimmings.

Each cookie: About 61 calories, 1 g protein, 8 g carbohydrate, 3 g total fat (2 g saturated), 13 mg cholesterol, 47 mg sodium.

Classic Sugar Cookies

Finnish Almond Cookies

The perfect partner for a cup of freshly brewed coffee, these crisp cookies are a Scandinavian favorite. Better yet, there's almost no fuss and muss because you roll them out, cut into rectangles, and top with sugar and almonds right on the baking sheet.

PREP: 25 MINUTES   BAKE: 12 MINUTES PER BATCH
MAKES 42 COOKIES

3/4 cup butter or margarine
   (1 1/2 sticks), softened
1/4 cup plus 2 tablespoons sugar
1 large egg, separated
1 teaspoon almond extract

2 cups all-purpose flour
1 tablespoon water (if necessary)
1 cup sliced blanched almonds
   (4 ounces)

1. Preheat oven to 375°F. In large bowl, with mixer at medium speed, beat butter and 1/4 cup sugar until light and fluffy. Beat in egg yolk and almond extract until blended. Reduce speed to low; gradually beat in flour. If dough is dry and crumbly, sprinkle with the water; beat just until blended. Divide dough in half.

2. Sprinkle large ungreased cookie sheet with flour (if your cookie sheet has rim on four sides, use it upside down). With floured rolling pin, on cookie sheet, roll 1 piece of dough into 10 1/2" by 9" rectangle. Lightly beat egg white. With pastry brush, brush dough with some egg white; sprinkle with half of almonds and 1 tablespoon sugar. Cut dough crosswise into seven 1 1/2-inch-wide strips; cut each strip crosswise into 3 pieces.

3. Bake until edges are lightly browned, 12 to 15 minutes. If any cookies have not browned around edges, return to oven and bake several minutes longer. With wide metal spatula, transfer cookies to wire rack to cool completely.

4. Repeat with remaining dough, almonds, and sugar.

Each cookie: About 73 calories, 1 g protein, 7 g carbohydrate, 5 g total fat (2 g saturated), 14 mg cholesterol, 35 mg sodium.

Lemon-Glazed Flowers

Former Associate Food Editor Lori Conforti got this recipe from her mother's nanny, Irmgard Kersten. You don't have to bake the whole recipe at once; the dough can be frozen for up to three months.

PREP: 45 MINUTES PLUS CHILLING   BAKE: 10 MINUTES PER BATCH
MAKES ABOUT 108 COOKIES

BUTTER COOKIES
1 1/2 cups butter or margarine
   (3 sticks), softened
1 1/3 cups granulated sugar
1/2 teaspoon salt
3 large eggs
4 1/2 cups all-purpose flour

LEMON GLAZE
1 1/2 cups confectioners' sugar
1/4 cup plus 1 teaspoon fresh lemon
   juice (from 1 to 2 lemons)

1. Prepare cookies: In large bowl, with mixer at low speed, beat butter, granulated sugar, and salt until blended. Increase speed to high; beat until creamy. At low speed, beat in eggs, one at a time, beating well after each addition. Gradually beat in flour just until blended.
2. Divide dough into 4 equal pieces; flatten each into a disk. Wrap each disk in plastic and refrigerate until dough is firm enough to roll, at least 2 hours.
3. Meanwhile, prepare glaze: In small bowl, whisk confectioners' sugar and lemon juice until smooth; cover and set aside.
4. Preheat oven to 350°F. On lightly floured surface, with floured rolling pin, roll 1 piece of dough 1/8 inch thick. With floured 2 1/2-inch round scalloped cookie cutter, cut dough into as many cookies as possible; wrap and refrigerate trimmings. With floured wide metal spatula, carefully place cookies, 1 inch apart, on ungreased large cookie sheet.
5. Bake cookies until lightly browned, 10 to 12 minutes. With wide metal spatula, transfer cookies to wire rack. Brush tops of warm cookies generously with glaze; cool on wire rack.
6. Repeat with remaining dough, trimmings, and glaze.

Each cookie: About 60 calories, 1 g protein, 8 g carbohydrate, 3 g total fat (2 g saturated), 13 mg cholesterol, 40 mg sodium.

Gingerbread Cutouts

Gingerbread Cutouts

Our whimsical ginger people are in good taste any time of the year. At Christmas this spicy dough is perfect for cutting into seasonal shapes or for constructing your own gingerbread house.

PREP: 45 MINUTE PLUS COOLING AND DECORATING
BAKE: 12 MINUTES PER BATCH
MAKES ABOUT 36 COOKIES

1/2 cup sugar	2 teaspoons baking soda
1/2 cup light (mild) molasses	1/2 cup butter or margarine
1 1/2 teaspoons ground ginger	(1 stick), cut into pieces
1 teaspoon ground allspice	1 large egg, beaten
1 teaspoon ground cinnamon	3 1/2 cups all-purpose flour
1 teaspoon ground cloves	Ornamental Frosting (see page 248)

1. In 3-quart saucepan, heat sugar, molasses, ginger, allspice, cinnamon, and cloves to boiling over medium heat, stirring occasionally with wooden spoon. Remove pan from heat; stir in baking soda (mixture will foam up in pan). Stir in butter until melted. Stir in egg. Add flour and stir until dough forms.

2. On floured surface, knead dough until combined. Divide dough in half; wrap 1 piece in waxed paper and refrigerate while working with remaining half.

3. Preheat oven to 325°F. On lightly floured surface, with floured rolling pin, roll 1 piece of dough a scant 1/4 inch thick. With floured 3- to 4-inch assorted cookie cutters, cut dough into as many cookies as possible; reserve trimmings. Place cookies, 1 inch apart, on ungreased large cookie sheet.

4. Bake until edges begin to brown, 12 minutes. With wide metal spatula, transfer cookies to wire racks to cool. Repeat with remaining dough and trimmings.

5. When cookies are cool, prepare Ornamental Frosting. Use frosting to decorate cookies; let dry completely, about 1 hour.

Each cookie without frosting: About 95 calories, 2 g protein, 16 g carbohydrate, 3 g total fat (2 g saturated), 13 mg cholesterol, 100 mg sodium.

Linzer Cookies

Freelance writer Delia Blackler's mother-in-law, Helgard Perretta, has been delighting neighbors and friends with her famous thin almond sandwich cookies for years, and she was generous enough to share her recipe with us. They are a good choice to pack and send.

PREP: 1 HOUR PLUS CHILLING AND COOLING
BAKE: 12 MINUTES PER BATCH
MAKES ABOUT 24 COOKIES

1/2 cup blanched almonds
1 cup granulated sugar
2 3/4 cups all-purpose flour
1 tablespoon freshly grated
   lemon peel
1/2 teaspoon baking powder
1/4 teaspoon salt
1 cup butter or margarine
   (2 sticks), softened

1 package (3 ounces) cream cheese,
   softened
1 large egg
confectioners' sugar
1/2 cup seedless red raspberry or
   other favorite jam

1. In food processor with knife blade attached, process almonds and 1/2 cup granulated sugar until almonds are finely ground. Add flour, lemon peel, baking powder, salt, and remaining 1/2 cup granulated sugar; pulse until evenly mixed. Add butter, cream cheese, and egg and process just until dough forms, occasionally stopping processor and scraping down side with rubber spatula.

2. Divide dough in half; flatten each half into a disk. Wrap each disk in plastic and refrigerate until dough is firm enough to roll, at least 2 hours.

3. Preheat oven to 350°F. On lightly floured surface, with floured rolling pin, roll 1 piece of dough 1/8 inch thick. With floured 3-inch fluted round cookie cutter, cut dough into as many rounds as possible. With 1-inch star or fluted round cookie cutter, cut out and remove centers from half of rounds. Reserve centers and trimmings to reroll. With lightly floured wide metal spatula, carefully place rounds, about 1 inch apart, on ungreased large cookie sheet.

4. Bake cookies until edges are lightly browned, 12 to 14 minutes. With wide metal spatula, transfer cookies to wire rack to cool completely. Repeat with remaining dough and reserved centers and trimmings.

5. When cookies are cool, sprinkle confectioners' sugar through sieve over cookies with cut-out centers. In small saucepan, melt jam over low heat, stirring frequently. Brush whole cookies with melted jam; top with cut-out cookies.

Each cookie: About 210 calories, 3 g protein, 25 g carbohydrate, 11 g total fat (6 g saturated), 35 mg cholesterol, 130 mg sodium.

Nutmeg Bells

Textiles Director Kathleen Huddy Sperduto brought us this recipe from her great-aunt Martha's repertoire of cookies. Although they are made for the holidays in the Sperduto home, their spicy nutmeg flavor is good any time of the year.

Prep: 1 Hour Plus Chilling, Cooling, And Decorating
Bake: 10 Minutes Per Batch
Makes About 66 Cookies

2 cups sugar
1 cup butter (2 sticks), softened (do not use margarine)
2 large eggs
2 teaspoons vanilla extract
3 1/2 cups all-purpose flour

4 teaspoons baking powder
1 teaspoon ground nutmeg
1 teaspoon salt
Ornamental Frosting (see page 248, optional)

1. In large bowl, with mixer at medium speed, beat sugar and butter until creamy, about 2 minutes. Reduce speed to low; beat in eggs and vanilla until blended. Gradually beat in flour, baking powder, nutmeg, and salt until well blended, occasionally scraping bowl with rubber spatula.

2. Divide dough into thirds; flatten each third into a disk. Wrap each disk in plastic and refrigerate until dough is firm enough to roll, at least 2 hours.

3. Preheat oven to 350°F. On lightly floured surface, with floured rolling pin, roll 1 piece of dough 1/8 inch thick. With floured 3 1/2-inch bell-shaped cookie cutter, cut dough into as many cookies as possible; wrap and refrigerate trimmings. Place cookies, 1 inch apart, on ungreased large cookie sheet.

4. Bake until lightly browned, 10 to 12 minutes. With wide metal spatula, transfer cookies to wire rack to cool. Repeat with remaining dough and trimmings.

5. When cookies are cool, prepare Ornamental Frosting, if you like. Use frosting to decorate cookies as desired (see box, page 249); let dry completely, about 1 hour.

Each cookie without frosting: About 75 calories, 1 g protein, 11 g carbohydrate, 3 g total fat (2 g saturated), 14 mg cholesterol, 90 mg sodium.

Pfeffernusse

These melt-in-your-mouth cookies from Carol A. Buck of Sherman Oaks, California, have a spicy orange flavor. Although *pfeffernusse* means "pepper nuts" in German, the cookies are more often spiced with cinnamon, cloves, and allspice, as they are here.

PREP: 1 HOUR 30 MINUTES PLUS CHILLING
BAKE: 8 MINUTES PER BATCH
MAKES ABOUT 240 COOKIES

2 cups sugar
3 large eggs
3 1/2 cups all-purpose flour
2 tablespoons freshly grated
  orange peel

1 teaspoon ground cinnamon
1 teaspoon ground allspice
1 teaspoon baking powder
1 teaspoon lemon extract
1/2 teaspoon ground cloves

1. In large bowl, with mixer at low speed, beat sugar and eggs until blended. Increase speed to high; beat until creamy. Reduce speed to low; add flour, orange peel, cinnamon, allspice, baking powder, lemon extract, and cloves and beat until well combined, occasionally scraping bowl with rubber spatula.

2. With lightly floured hands, shape dough into 4 balls; flatten each slightly. Wrap each ball in plastic and refrigerate overnight. (Dough will be very sticky even after chilling.)

3. Preheat oven to 400°F. Grease large cookie sheet. On well-floured surface, with floured rolling pin, roll 1 piece of dough into 10" by 6" rectangle; keep remaining dough in refrigerator. With floured pastry wheel or sharp knife, cut dough lengthwise into 6 strips, then cut each strip crosswise into 10 pieces. Place cookies, about 1/2 inch apart, on prepared cookie sheet.

4. Bake until lightly browned, 8 to 10 minutes. With wide metal spatula, transfer cookies to wire racks to cool.

5. Repeat with remaining dough.

Each cookie: About 15 calories, 0 g protein, 3 g carbohydrate, 0 g total fat, 4 mg cholesterol, 5 mg sodium.

Pinwheels

Pinwheels

You'll be surprised at how easy it is to shape these pretty treats. For variety in both flavor and color, try using several different kinds of jam.

PREP: 35 MINUTES PLUS CHILLING   BAKE: 9 MINUTES PER BATCH
MAKES 24 COOKIES

1 1/3 cups all-purpose flour
1/4 teaspoon baking powder
1/8 teaspoon salt
6 tablespoons butter or margarine, softened

1/2 cup sugar
1 large egg
1 teaspoon vanilla extract
1/4 cup Damson plum, seedless raspberry, or other jam

1. In small bowl, stir together flour, baking powder, and salt.

2. In large bowl, with mixer at medium speed, beat butter and sugar until light and fluffy. Beat in egg and vanilla until combined. Reduce speed to low and beat in flour mixture just until combined. Divide dough in half. Wrap each half in waxed paper and refrigerate until firm enough to roll, at least 1 hour or overnight. (If using margarine, freeze overnight.)

3. Preheat oven to 375°F. On floured surface, with floured rolling pin, roll 1 piece of dough into 10" by 7 1/2" rectangle; keep remaining dough refrigerated. With fluted pastry wheel or sharp knife, cut into twelve 2 1/2-inch squares. Place 1 square at a time, 1 inch apart, on two ungreased cookie sheets. Make a 1 1/2-inch cut from each corner toward center. Spoon 1/2 teaspoon jam in center of each square. Fold every other tip in to center. Repeat with remaining squares.

4. Bake until edges are lightly browned and cookies are set, 9 minutes, rotating sheets between upper and lower racks halfway through baking. With wide metal spatula, transfer to wire racks to cool completely.

5. Repeat with remaining dough and jam.

Each cookie: About 80 calories, 1 g protein, 12 g carbohydrate, 3 g total fat (2 g saturated), 17 mg cholesterol, 50 mg sodium.

Rugelach

There are many varieties of this Eastern European specialty, but rugelach are always made with cream cheese and have the same characteristic crescent shape. They are wonderful make-aheads, because you can shape them and freeze for up to a month. Then just pop them in the oven still frozen, and they'll bake up perfectly.

PREP: 1 HOUR PLUS CHILLING   BAKE: 30 MINUTES
MAKES 48 RUGELACH

1 cup butter or margarine (2 sticks), softened
1 package (8 ounces) cream cheese, softened
1 tablespoon plus 1/2 cup sugar
1 teaspoon vanilla extract
1 teaspoon freshly grated orange peel (optional)

2 cups all-purpose flour
1 1/2 teaspoons ground cinnamon
8 teaspoons butter, melted
1 cup walnuts, chopped
1 cup dried currants
1 large egg yolk
1 tablespoon water

1. In large bowl, with mixer at low speed, beat butter and cream cheese until blended and creamy. Beat in 1 tablespoon sugar, vanilla, and orange peel, if using. Beat in flour until blended. Divide dough into 4 equal pieces. Wrap each piece in waxed paper and refrigerate until firm enough to roll, at least 2 hours or overnight. (If using margarine, freeze overnight.)

2. Preheat oven to 325°F. Line two large cookie sheets with foil; grease foil. In small bowl, stir together cinnamon and remaining 1/2 cup sugar.

3. On lightly floured surface, with floured rolling pin, roll 1 piece of chilled dough into 10 1/2-inch round; keeping remaining dough refrigerated. Brush dough with 2 teaspoons melted butter. Sprinkle generous 2 tablespoons cinnamon-sugar mixture over dough. Sprinkle one-fourth of nuts and one-fourth of currants over top; gently press filling into dough.

4. With pastry wheel or sharp knife, cut dough into 12 equal wedges. Starting at curved edge, roll up each wedge, jelly-roll fashion (see photo, page 143). Place cookies, point side down, 1/2 inch apart, on prepared cookie sheets; shape into crescents. Repeat with remaining dough, melted butter, and fillings, one-fourth at a time.

5. Preheat oven to 325°F. In cup, stir together egg yolk and water. With pastry brush, lightly brush egg-yolk mixture over rugelach.

6. Bake until golden, 30 minutes, rotating cookie sheets between upper and lower oven racks halfway through baking. With wide metal spatula, immediately transfer rugelach to wire racks to cool completely.

Each rugelach: About 110 calories, 1 g protein, 9 g carbohydrate, 8 g total fat (4 g saturated), 22 mg cholesterol, 60 mg sodium.

Apricot-Raspberry Rugelach

Here, we give classic rugelach a new twist.

PREP: 1 HOUR PLUS CHILLING   BAKE: 35 MINUTES
MAKES 48 RUGELACH

1 cup butter or margarine (2 sticks),
  softened
1 package (8 ounces) cream cheese,
  softened
3/4 cup granulated sugar
1 teaspoon vanilla extract
1/4 teaspoon salt

2 cups all-purpose flour
1 cup walnuts (4 ounces), chopped
3/4 cup dried apricots, chopped
1/4 cup packed light brown sugar
1 1/2 teaspoons ground cinnamon
1/2 cup seedless raspberry preserves
1 tablespoon milk

1. In large bowl, with mixer at low speed, beat butter and cream cheese until creamy. Beat in 1/4 cup granulated sugar, vanilla, and salt. Beat in 1 cup flour. With wooden spoon, stir in remaining 1 cup flour just until blended. Divide dough into 4 equal pieces; flatten each into a disk. Wrap each disk in waxed paper and refrigerate until firm, at least 2 hours.

2. In medium bowl, combine walnuts, apricots, brown sugar, 1/4 cup plus 2 tablespoons granulated sugar, and 1/2 teaspoon cinnamon until well mixed. Line two large cookie sheets with foil; grease foil.

3. On lightly floured surface, with floured rolling pin, roll 1 disk of dough into 9-inch round; keep remaining dough refrigerated. Spread 2 tablespoons preserves over dough. Sprinkle with 1/2 cup walnut mixture; gently press to adhere. With pastry wheel or sharp knife, cut dough into 12 equal wedges. Starting at curved edge, roll up each wedge, jelly-roll fashion. Place cookies, point side down, 1/2 inch apart, on prepared cookie sheets; shape into crescents. Repeat with remaining dough, one-fourth at a time.

4. Preheat oven to 325°F. In cup, combine remaining 2 tablespoons granulated sugar and remaining 1 teaspoon cinnamon. With pastry brush, brush rugelach with milk. Sprinkle evenly with cinnamon-sugar.

5. Bake until golden, 35 to 40 minutes, rotating cookie sheets between upper and lower oven racks halfway through baking. With wide metal spatula, immediately transfer rugelach to wire racks to cool completely.

Each rugelach: About 116 calories, 1 g protein, 12 g carbohydrate, 7 g total fat (4 g saturated), 16 mg cholesterol, 67 mg sodium.

CUTTING AND SHAPING RUGELACH

After spreading the filling on rugelach dough, cut into wedges
using a pastry wheel or a sharp knife.

Starting from wide end, roll up rugelach wedges. Place with the point
down and shape into a crescent.

Shortcut Rugelach

In a hurry for something sweet? These quick rugelach don't look quite the same as the traditional ones, but you can thaw the puff pastry on the way home from the supermarket and have them in the oven in a snap.

Prep: 35 Minutes Plus Thawing And Cooling
Bake: 15 Minutes Per Batch
Makes 48 Cookies

1 package (17 1/4 ounces) frozen
  puff-pastry sheets
1 cup dark seedless raisins
2/3 cup walnuts

2/3 cup plus 2 teaspoons sugar
1 teaspoon ground cinnamon
1 large egg white
1 teaspoon water

1. Remove 1 puff-pastry sheet from freezer; let stand at room temperature about 20 minutes to thaw as label directs.

2. While pastry is thawing, in food processor with knife blade attached, process raisins, walnuts, 2/3 cup sugar, and 3/4 teaspoon cinnamon until raisins and walnuts are finely chopped.

3. In small bowl, lightly beat egg white and water. In another small bowl, mix remaining 2 teaspoons sugar and remaining 1/4 teaspoon cinnamon. Set both bowls aside.

4. Preheat oven to 375°F. Grease large cookie sheet. Remove second puff-pastry sheet from freezer; thaw as above.

5. Meanwhile, on lightly floured surface, with floured rolling pin, roll thawed puff-pastry sheet into 14" by 12" rectangle. Cut pastry crosswise in half to make two 7" by 12" rectangles. Divide raisin mixture into fourths. Sprinkle one-fourth of raisin mixture (rounded 1/2 cup) on 1 rectangle, leaving 3/4-inch border along a 12-inch side. Repeat with another one-fourth of the raisin mixture on second rectangle. Lightly brush border of each rectangle with some egg-white mixture. Roll each rectangle, jelly-roll fashion, starting from 12-inch side with filling; pinch seam to seal.

6. Brush rolls with egg-white mixture and sprinkle with half of cinnamon-sugar. Cut each roll crosswise into 12 (about 1-inch-thick) pieces. Place pieces, about 1 1/2 inches apart, seam side down, on prepared cookie sheet. Bake until puffed and golden, 15 to 17 minutes. With wide metal spatula, transfer rugelach to wire rack to cool.
7. Repeat, using second puff-pastry sheet and remaining ingredients.

Each rugelach: About 90 calories, 1 g protein, 10 g carbohydrate, 5 g total fat (1 g saturated), 0 mg cholesterol, 25 mg sodium.

Sour-Cream Nut Rolls

Freelance writer Kathleen Renda's mom, Rose, gave us this recipe for her special yeast-raised nut rolls. For convenience, you can raise the shaped rolls in the refrigerator overnight.

PREP: 50 MINUTES PLUS STANDING AND COOLING   BAKE: 40 MINUTES
MAKES ABOUT 48 COOKIES

WALNUT FILLING
2 1/2 cups walnuts, toasted
  (see page 73) and cooled
3/4 cup sugar
2 tablespoons butter or margarine,
  melted
1 tablespoon vanilla extract
2 teaspoons freshly grated
  orange peel
1/4 teaspoon salt

SOUR-CREAM DOUGH
1/4 cup warm water (105° to 115°F)
1 package active dry yeast
1 teaspoon plus 1/4 cup sugar
3 cups all-purpose flour
3/4 teaspoon salt
1/2 cup butter or margarine (1 stick),
  melted
1/2 cup sour cream
1 large egg plus 1 large egg, separated

1. Prepare filling: In food processor with knife blade attached, process walnuts, sugar, butter, vanilla, orange peel, and salt until walnuts are finely ground; set aside.

2. Prepare dough: In small bowl, combine warm water, yeast, and 1 teaspoon sugar; let stand until foamy, about 5 minutes.

3. In large bowl, stir together flour, remaining 1/4 cup sugar, and salt. Stir in butter, sour cream, 1 egg, 1 egg yolk, and yeast mixture until evenly moistened. (Cover and refrigerate remaining egg white.) With floured hands, knead dough in bowl a few times until dough comes together (dough will be sticky). Cover bowl with plastic wrap; let dough stand 10 minutes.

4. Divide dough in half. On lightly floured surface, with floured rolling pin, roll 1 piece of dough into 14" by 12" rectangle. Sprinkle half of filling evenly over dough; gently press filling into dough.

5. Starting from one long side of dough rectangle, tightly roll dough jellyroll fashion. Place roll, seam side down, on one side of ungreased large cookie sheet. Repeat with remaining dough and filling. Place second roll, 4 inches from first roll, on same cookie sheet. Cover rolls with plastic wrap

and let rise in warm place (80° to 85°F) 1 hour. If you like, instead of setting rolls aside to rise for 1 hour, refrigerate rolls, on cookie sheet, overnight. When ready to bake, let stand at room temperature 30 minutes before completing Steps 6 and 7.

6. Preheat oven to 325°F. Bake rolls 35 minutes.

7. Meanwhile in cup, lightly beat egg white. Brush rolls with egg white. Bake until golden, 5 minutes longer. With wide metal spatula, transfer rolls to wire rack to cool.

8. When rolls are cool, with serrated knife, cut crosswise into 1/2-inch-thick slices.

Each cookie: About 115 calories, 2 g protein, 11 g carbohydrate, 7 g total fat (2 g saturated), 17 mg cholesterol, 80 mg sodium.

Sour-Cream Cut-Out Cookies

A sprinkle of sugar makes these beautiful cookies sparkle. When rerolling the trimmings, press the pieces together to make a flattened rectangle rather than knead them together—the cookies will be more tender.

PREP: 35 MINUTES PLUS CHILLING   BAKE: 8 MINUTES PER BATCH
MAKES ABOUT 76 COOKIES

1 3/4 cups all-purpose flour
1/2 teaspoon baking soda
1/4 teaspoon salt
1/2 cup butter or margarine (1 stick), softened

1 cup plus about 2 tablespoons sugar
1 large egg
1 teaspoon vanilla extract
1/2 cup sour cream

1. In medium bowl, stir together flour, baking soda, and salt. In large bowl, with mixer at medium speed, beat butter and 1 cup sugar until combined. Reduce speed to low and beat in egg and vanilla until blended. Beat in sour cream. Beat in flour mixture until combined, scraping bowl occasionally with rubber spatula.

2. Divide dough into 4 balls; flatten each slightly. Wrap each in waxed paper and refrigerate until dough is firm enough to roll, at least 2 hours or overnight. (If using margarine, refrigerate overnight.)

3. Preheat oven to 350°F. On lightly floured surface, with floured rolling pin, roll 1 piece of dough 1/8 inch thick, keeping remaining dough refrigerated. With floured 2-inch cookie cutters, cut out as many cookies as possible; reserve trimmings. Place cookies, about 1 1/2 inches apart, on ungreased large cookie sheet. Sprinkle with some of remaining sugar.

4. Bake 8 minutes. With wide metal spatula, transfer cookies to wire racks to cool completely.

5. Repeat with remaining dough, trimmings, and sugar.

Each cookie: About 35 calories, 0 g protein, 5 g carbohydrate, 2 g total fat (1 g saturated), 7 mg cholesterol, 30 mg sodium.

ROVER'S REWARD

H ere's a healthy snack you can bake for your "best friend." Use a bone-shaped cookie cutter, or just cut into bars before baking.

PREP: 1 HOUR PLUS COOLING   BAKE: 30 TO 40 MINUTES PLUS DRYING
MAKES ABOUT 48 LARGE BISCUITS OR 288 SMALL BISCUITS

1/2 cup warm water (105° to 115°F)
1 package active dry yeast
1 teaspoon sugar
2 cups all-purpose flour
2 cups whole-wheat flour
2 cups cornmeal
2 cups old-fashioned oats, uncooked

1 cup loosely packed fresh mint leaves, chopped
1 cup loosely packed fresh parsley leaves, chopped
1/2 cup toasted wheat germ
1 can (13 3/4 to 14 1/2 ounces) beef broth
3/4 cup milk

1. Preheat oven to 350°F. In small bowl, combine warm water, yeast, and sugar; let stand until yeast foams, about 5 minutes.

2. In very large bowl, combine all-purpose flour, whole-wheat flour, cornmeal, oats, mint, parsley, and wheat germ. With wooden spoon, stir in yeast mixture, broth, and milk until combined. With hands, knead dough in bowl until blended, about 1 minute.

3. Divide dough in half. Cover 1 piece with plastic wrap to prevent it from drying out. Place remaining piece of dough on lightly floured surface. With floured rolling pin, roll dough 1/4 inch thick. With large (about 5 inches) or small (about 2 inches) cookie cutter, such as bone or mailman shape, cut out as many biscuits as possible; reserve trimmings. With wide metal spatula, transfer biscuits to large ungreased cookie sheet. Reroll trimmings and cut more biscuits. Repeat with remaining dough.

4. Bake small biscuits 30 minutes; bake large biscuits 40 minutes. Turn oven off; leave biscuits in oven 1 hour to dry out.

5. Transfer biscuits from cookie sheet to wire rack. When cool, store at room temperature in tightly covered container up to 3 months.

Each large biscuit: About 90 calories, 4 g protein, 17 g carbohydrate, 1 g total fat (0 g saturated), 1 mg cholesterol, 30 mg sodium.

Spice Thins

Associate Food Director Debby Goldsmith learned to make these crisp, buttery, Swedish cookies from her childhood nanny, Anna. The family-size recipe makes almost eight dozen cookies, but Debby says that they keep very, very well.

PREP: 45 MINUTES PLUS CHILLING AND COOLING
BAKE: 10 MINUTES PER BATCH
MAKES ABOUT 90 COOKIES

1 cup butter (2 sticks), softened (do not use margarine)	2 1/2 teaspoons baking soda
1 cup sugar	2 teaspoons ground cinnamon
1/2 cup dark corn syrup	2 teaspoons ground cloves
1/2 cup heavy or whipping cream	2 teaspoons ground ginger
	4 cups all-purpose flour

1. In large bowl, with mixer at low speed, beat butter and sugar until blended. Increase speed to high; beat until light and creamy, occasionally scraping bowl with rubber spatula. Reduce speed to low; beat in corn syrup, cream, baking soda, cinnamon, cloves, and ginger until blended. Gradually beat in flour until well mixed.

2. Divide dough into 8 pieces. Wrap each piece in plastic and refrigerate overnight.

3. Preheat oven to 350°F. On lightly floured surface, with floured rolling pin, roll 1 piece of dough 1/8 inch thick, keeping remaining dough refrigerated. With floured 3-inch round fluted cookie cutter, cut dough into as many cookies as possible; reserve trimmings. Place cookies, 1 inch apart, on ungreased large cookie sheet.

4. Bake until lightly browned, 10 to 12 minutes. With wide metal spatula, transfer cookies to wire rack to cool.

5. Repeat with remaining dough and trimmings.

Each cookie: About 55 calories, 1 g protein, 8 g carbohydrate, 3 g total fat (2 g saturated), 7 mg cholesterol, 60 mg sodium.

Simple Sugar Cookies

This recipe is so easy, so good, and so perfect for so many different occasions, that you might want to bake a double batch and freeze half. To freeze baked undecorated cookies, thoroughly cool them, then pack cookies in a sturdy, airtight container separated by waxed paper. To thaw them, unwrap the cookies and let them stand for about ten minutes at room temperature.

PREP: 30 MINUTES PLUS CHILLING   BAKE: 9 MINUTES PER BATCH
MAKES ABOUT 60 COOKIES

2 cups all-purpose flour	1 cup sugar
1/2 teaspoon baking powder	1 large egg
1/4 teaspoon salt	1 teaspoon vanilla extract
1/2 cup butter (1 stick), softened	

1. In medium bowl, stir together flour, baking powder, and salt.

2. With mixer at medium speed, beat butter and sugar until light and fluffy. Beat in egg and vanilla. Reduce speed to low and beat in flour mixture until blended. Divide dough in half. Wrap each half in waxed paper and refrigerate at least 1 hour or overnight.

3. Preheat oven to 375°F. On lightly floured surface, with floured rolling pin, roll 1 piece of dough 1/8 inch thick. With 2 1/2-inch cookie cutters, cut dough into as many cookies as possible; reserve trimmings. Place cookies, 1 inch apart, on two ungreased large cookie sheets.

4. Bake until lightly browned, 9 to 10 minutes, rotating cookie sheets between upper and lower oven racks halfway through baking. Cool on cookie sheets on wire racks 1 minute. With wide metal spatula, transfer cookies to wire racks to cool completely.

5. Repeat with remaining dough and trimmings.

Each cookie: About 45 calories, 1 g protein, 7 g carbohydrate, 2 g total fat (1 g saturated), 8 mg cholesterol, 30 mg sodium.

PRESSED, MOLDED, & REFRIGERATOR COOKIES

Whether shaped, sliced, curled, or twisted, molded cookies are almost as much fun to make as they are to eat. Children love to help shape the balls and crescents, but no matter what your age, there is something satisfying about creating with your hands. Many of the cookies in this chapter have traditions of long standing. Carried to America from a variety of homelands, they now appear together in cookie tins across the country, especially at the holidays. Refrigerator cookies, often called icebox cookies, became the "rage"— and the first convenience food—in the late nineteenth century, when women discovered that having a roll of cookie dough in the icebox meant they could serve warm cookies at a moment's notice. This time-saver is just as useful today.

Although these are a little trickier than drop and bar cookies, you should be able to get delicious results if you follow these easy tips.

• *Work quickly with each ball of dough.* You can start shaping the dough as soon as it is made because molded cookie dough is usually stiff enough so that it doesn't require chilling. But move fast so that the heat of your hands doesn't melt the butter in it and make it sticky.

• *If the dough begins to stick* to your hands, rubbing your hands with a little flour or vegetable oil will help.

• *If the dough starts to get crumbly*, moisten your hands with water. It will make the cookies easier to shape.

• *Follow cookie press directions carefully*, especially when making spritz cookies, as all of them have slightly different instructions.

• *To freeze dough* just wrap it tightly in heavy-duty foil and pack in an air-tight container. It will keep frozen for three months. Be sure to thaw the dough in the refrigerator, and remember to label each package with the contents and date.

Anisette Cookies

Ann Cullen of Wantagh, New York, sent us this old-fashioned Italian cookie recipe, which she received from her sister Theresa. Both the dough and the glaze are flavored with anisette.

PREP: 1 HOUR PLUS CHILLING AND COOLING
BAKE: 12 MINUTES PER BATCH
MAKES 36 COOKIES

1/2 cup margarine or butter
(1 stick), softened
1/2 cup granulated sugar
3 large eggs
1 teaspoon vanilla extract
2 teaspoons anise extract or anisette
(anise-flavored liqueur)

2 1/2 cups all-purpose flour
1 tablespoon baking powder
3/4 cup confectioners' sugar
2 tablespoons water
red and green sprinkles (optional)

1. In large bowl, with mixer at low speed, beat margarine and granulated sugar until blended. Increase speed to high; beat until creamy. At medium speed, beat in eggs, vanilla, and 1 teaspoon anise extract, constantly scraping bowl with rubber spatula. Reduce speed to low; beat in flour and baking powder, occasionally scraping bowl. Shape dough into 4 balls. Wrap each ball in plastic and freeze at least 1 hour or refrigerate overnight.

2. Preheat oven to 350°F. On lightly floured surface, divide 1 ball of dough into 9 equal pieces; keep remaining dough refrigerated. With lightly floured hands, roll each piece of dough into a 7-inch-long rope; gently twist several times. Bring ends of rope together and pinch to seal.

3. Place cookies, about 2 inches apart, on ungreased large cookie sheet. Bake until bottoms are lightly browned, 12 minutes. With wide metal spatula, transfer cookies to wire rack to cool. Repeat with remaining dough.

4. When cookies are cool, prepare glaze: In small bowl, mix confectioners' sugar, remaining 1 teaspoon anise extract, and water. With pastry brush, brush tops of cookies with glaze; place on rack. Top with sprinkles, if you like. Set cookies aside to allow glaze to dry, about 1 hour.

Each cookie without sprinkles: About 80 calories, 1 g protein, 12 g carbohydrate, 3 g total fat (1 g saturated), 18 mg cholesterol, 70 mg sodium.

Almond Leaves

To make these lovely cookies in the traditional leaf shape, you will need a stencil spatula that has a leaf-shaped cutout in the center. However, they taste just as delicious if you drop teaspoons of batter on cool buttered trays and spread it into rounds or free-form shapes.

PREP: 65 MINUTES PLUS COOLING   BAKE: 7 MINUTES PER BATCH
MAKES ABOUT 36 COOKIES

1/3 cup almond paste (3 1/2 ounces), crumbled	1 large egg, slightly beaten
1/4 cup sugar	1/4 teaspoon almond extract
3 tablespoons butter or margarine, softened	1/3 cup plus 2 tablespoons all-purpose flour

1. Preheat oven to 350°F. In small bowl, with mixer at medium speed, beat almond paste until softened. Add sugar and beat until smooth (a few small lumps will remain). Add butter and beat until well blended. Reduce speed to low and beat in egg and almond extract until incorporated. Stir in flour until just combined, scraping bowl occasionally with rubber spatula.

2. Generously butter two large cookie sheets. Spread batter by teaspoonfuls through leaf spatula on prepared cookie sheets and smooth 1/8 inch thick with small wet metal spatula. Repeat with some of remaining batter, leaving 2 inches between leaves.

3. Bake until edges are golden, 7 to 9 minutes, rotating sheets between upper and lower racks halfway through baking. With wide metal spatula, transfer cookies to wire rack to cool completely.

4. Repeat with remaining batter.

Each cookie: About 35 calories, 1 g protein, 4 g carbohydrate, 2 g total fat (1 g saturated), 9 mg cholesterol, 15 mg sodium.

Chocolate Almond Leaves: Prepare as above; cool. Melt *3 1/2 squares (3 1/2 ounces) semisweet chocolate.* Spread chocolate in thin layer over cooled cookies, marking veins of leaves with edge of small metal spatula. Let stand on wire racks until chocolate has set.

Each cookie: About 50 calories, 1 g protein, 6 g carbohydrate, 3 g total fat (1 g saturated), 9 mg cholesterol, 15 mg sodium.

Almond Leaves

Chocolate Crinkles

This cookie takes its name from its interesting shape. As the sugar-coated rich dough bakes, it spreads into puffy rounds with small furrows. It makes a luscious addition to any lunch box or cookie tray.

PREP: 25 MINUTES PLUS CHILLING   BAKE: 8 MINUTES PER BATCH
MAKES ABOUT 96 COOKIES

1 3/4 cups all-purpose flour
1/2 cup unsweetened cocoa
1 teaspoon baking soda
1/2 teaspoon baking powder
1/4 teaspoon salt
1/2 cup butter or margarine
   (1 stick), softened

1 1/4 cups granulated sugar
2 tablespoons light corn syrup
2 squares (2 ounces) unsweetened
   chocolate, melted and cooled
2 large eggs
2 teaspoons vanilla extract
1/2 cup confectioners' sugar

1. In small bowl, stir together flour, cocoa, baking soda, baking powder, and salt.

2. In large bowl, with mixer at medium speed, beat butter, granulated sugar, and corn syrup until combined. Reduce speed to low and beat in chocolate, eggs, and vanilla until well blended. Beat in flour mixture until combined, scraping bowl occasionally with rubber spatula. Cover dough and refrigerate 1 hour.

3. Preheat oven to 350°F. Place confectioners' sugar in small bowl. Shape dough by level teaspoons into 1-inch balls; roll in confectioners' sugar.

4. Place cookies, 1 inch apart, on ungreased large cookie sheet. Bake until set, about 8 minutes. With wide metal spatula, transfer cookies to wire rack to cool completely.

5. Repeat with remaining dough and confectioners' sugar.

Each cookie: About 35 calories, 1 g protein, 6 g carbohydrate, 1 g total fat (1 g saturated), 7 mg cholesterol, 35 mg sodium.

Chocolate Sambuca Cookies

This seriously chocolate cookie, spiked with sambuca liqueur, makes an elegant after-dinner confection. Leslie R. Husted of Clinton, New York, got the recipe from a friend and looks forward to baking them frequently.

PREP: 30 MINUTES PLUS CHILLING
BAKE: 10 MINUTES PER BATCH
MAKES ABOUT 48 COOKIES

12 squares (12 ounces) semisweet chocolate, chopped
4 tablespoons margarine or butter ($1/2$ stick)
3 large eggs
$1/3$ cup sambuca (anise-flavored liqueur)

1 cup granulated sugar
1 cup blanched almonds, finely ground
$2/3$ cup all-purpose flour
$3/4$ teaspoon baking soda
$1/3$ cup confectioners' sugar

1. In 2-quart saucepan, melt chocolate and margarine over low heat, stirring frequently, until smooth. Remove saucepan from heat; cool chocolate mixture slightly.
2. In medium bowl, with wire whisk, mix eggs, sambuca, and $1/2$ cup granulated sugar; blend in chocolate mixture.
3. With spoon, stir ground almonds, flour, and baking soda into chocolate mixture until combined (dough will be very soft). Cover bowl with plastic wrap and refrigerate at least 4 hours or overnight.
4. Preheat oven to 350°F. In small bowl, combine confectioners' sugar and remaining $1/2$ cup granulated sugar. With lightly floured hands, roll dough by rounded tablespoons into balls. Roll balls in sugar mixture to coat. Place balls, about 2 inches apart, on ungreased large cookie sheet.
5. Bake until cookies are just set and look puffed and cracked, 10 to 12 minutes. Cool on cookie sheet on wire rack 1 minute. With wide metal spatula, transfer cookies to wire rack to cool completely.
6. Repeat with remaining dough and sugar mixture.

Each cookie: About 85 calories, 2 g protein, 12 g carbohydrate, 4 g total fat (0 g saturated), 13 mg cholesterol, 20 mg sodium.

Chocolate-Coconut Bites

Chocolate lovers will come running when they smell these coconut-studded cookies baking in the oven. Fortunately, the bite-size morsels are ready to eat as soon as they are cool enough to hold.

PREP: 30 MINUTES PLUS CHILLING   BAKE: 12 MINUTES PER BATCH
MAKES ABOUT 48 COOKIES

8 squares (8 ounces) semisweet chocolate, chopped	1/4 teaspoon salt
6 tablespoons butter or margarine (3/4 stick), cut into pieces	3/4 cup sugar
	2 teaspoons vanilla extract
1/3 cup all-purpose flour	2 large eggs
1/4 cup unsweetened cocoa	1 package (6 ounces) semisweet chocolate chips (1 cup)
1/2 teaspoon baking powder	1 cup flaked sweetened coconut

1. In 1-quart saucepan, melt chopped chocolate and butter over low heat, stirring occasionally, until smooth. Pour melted chocolate mixture into large bowl; cool to lukewarm, about 10 minutes.

2. Meanwhile, in small bowl, combine flour, cocoa, baking powder, and salt.

3. Stir sugar and vanilla into chocolate mixture until blended. Mix in eggs, one at a time. Add flour mixture, chocolate chips, and coconut and stir until combined. Cover with plastic wrap and refrigerate 1 hour.

4. Preheat oven to 350°F. Shape dough into 1 1/2-inch balls. Place balls, 2 inches apart, on ungreased large cookie sheet.

5. Bake until set, 12 to 14 minutes. Cool on cookie sheet on wire rack 2 minutes. With wide metal spatula, carefully transfer cookies to wire rack to cool completely. Clean edge of spatula after each batch, if necessary, for easier removal of cookies from cookie sheet.

6. Repeat with remaining dough.

Each cookie: About 85 calories, 1 g protein, 10 g carbohydrate, 5 g total fat (3 g saturated), 13 mg cholesterol, 40 mg sodium.

Jumbo Gingersnaps

We like our soft, chewy gingersnaps extra big, but you can make them smaller if you prefer. Be sure to cool the cookies briefly on the cookie sheet before moving them to racks, as they are very moist and soft when hot and could fall apart.

PREP: 20 MINUTES   BAKE: 15 MINUTES

MAKES 10 GIANT COOKIES OR ABOUT 30 SMALL COOKIES

2 cups all-purpose flour
2 teaspoons ground ginger
1 teaspoon baking soda
1/2 teaspoon ground cinnamon
1/2 teaspoon salt
1/4 teaspoon ground black pepper
(optional)

3/4 cup vegetable shortening
1/2 cup plus 2 tablespoons sugar
1 large egg
1/2 cup dark molasses

1. Preheat oven to 350°F. In medium bowl, combine flour, ginger, baking soda, cinnamon, salt, and pepper, if using.

2. In large bowl, with mixer at medium speed, beat shortening and 1/2 cup sugar until light and fluffy. Beat in egg until blended; beat in molasses. Reduce speed to low; beat in flour mixture just until blended.

3. Place remaining 2 tablespoons sugar on sheet of waxed paper. Roll 1/4 cup dough into ball; roll in sugar to coat evenly. Repeat with remaining dough to make 10 balls in all. Place balls, 3 inches apart, on ungreased large cookie sheet. Or, for small cookies, roll dough by slightly rounded tablespoons into balls and place 2 inches apart on two ungreased cookie sheets.

4. Bake until set, about 15 minutes for large cookies or 9 to 11 minutes for smaller cookies, rotating cookie sheets between upper and lower oven racks halfway through baking. Cookies will be very soft and may appear moist in cracks. Cool 1 minute on cookie sheets on wire racks; with wide metal spatula, transfer cookies to wire racks to cool completely.

Each giant cookie: About 323 calories, 3 g protein, 42 g carbohydrate, 16 g total fat (4 g saturated), 21 mg cholesterol, 258 mg sodium.

Sugar Twists

Children will love to help shape these sparkly cookies. For variety, you can use different-colored sugars or a drizzle of melted white chocolate in place of the white sugar crystals.

PREP: 1 HOUR PLUS CHILLING   BAKE: 11 MINUTES PER BATCH
MAKES 120 COOKIES

1 1/3 cups all-purpose flour
1/2 teaspoon baking soda
1/2 teaspoon salt
4 large eggs
1 1/2 cups granulated sugar

1 cup butter (2 sticks), softened
   (do not use margarine)
2 teaspoons vanilla extract
white sugar crystals (optional)

1. In small bowl, combine flour, baking soda, and salt. Separate 2 eggs, placing yolks in small bowl and whites in another. Cover and refrigerate whites; reserve for brushing on cookies later.

2. In large bowl, with mixer at medium speed, beat granulated sugar and butter until creamy, occasionally scraping bowl with rubber spatula. Beat in whole eggs, egg yolks, and vanilla. Reduce speed to low; gradually beat in flour mixture until blended.

3. Divide dough into 4 equal pieces. Wrap each piece in plastic wrap and refrigerate until dough is firm enough to roll, at least 2 hours. (Or place dough in freezer for 30 minutes.)

4. Preheat oven to 350°F. Grease large cookie sheet.

5. On lightly floured surface with floured hands, press 1 piece of dough into 6" by 3" by 3/4" rectangle; keep remaining dough refrigerated. Cut rectangle into 30 equal pieces. Roll each piece into a 6-inch-long rope. Transfer 1 rope at a time to prepared cookie sheet; gently shape into a loop, with ends overlapping. Repeat with remaining ropes, placing cookies 1 inch apart. Brush cookies with reserved egg whites; sprinkle with sugar crystals, if you like.

6. Bake until lightly browned, 11 to 12 minutes. With wide metal spatula, transfer cookies to wire rack to cool.

7. Repeat with remaining dough, egg whites, and sugar crystals, if using.

Each cookie: About 41 calories, 1 g protein, 5 g carbohydrate, 2 g total fat (1 g saturated), 12 mg cholesterol, 36 mg sodium.

Fortune Cookies

With our homemade fortune cookies, you can have fun personalizing the fortunes for special occasions. The secret to shaping the cookies is to bake only two at a time and to fold them quickly while still hot.

PREP: 45 MINUTES   BAKE: 4 MINUTES PER BATCH
MAKES ABOUT 14 COOKIES

2 tablespoons butter (do not use
  margarine)
1/4 cup confectioners' sugar
1 large egg white
1 teaspoon vanilla extract
pinch salt

1/4 cup all-purpose flour
14 strips paper (3" by 1/2" each)
  with fortunes

1. Preheat oven to 375°F. Grease two small cookie sheets.
2. In 1-quart saucepan, heat butter over low heat until melted. Remove saucepan from heat. With wire whisk, beat in confectioners' sugar, egg white, vanilla, and salt until blended. Beat in flour until batter is smooth.
3. Drop 1 heaping teaspoon batter onto cookie sheet. Repeat with another teaspoon batter, at least 4 inches away from first. With small metal spatula or back of spoon, spread batter evenly to form two 3-inch rounds.
4. Bake until cookies are lightly golden, about 4 minutes. Loosen both cookies with metal spatula. Working with 1 cookie at a time, place a fortune across center of hot cookie. Fold hot cookie in half, forming a semicircle, and press edges together. Quickly fold semicircle over edge of small bowl to create fortune-cookie shape. Repeat with remaining cookie. Let shaped cookies cool completely on wire rack.
5. Repeat with remaining batter and strips of fortune paper to make 14 cookies in all, cooling cookie sheets between batches and regreasing sheets as necessary.

Each cookie: About 35 calories, 1 g protein, 4 g carbohydrate, 2 g total fat (1 g saturated), 4 mg cholesterol, 30 mg sodium.

Shaping Fortune Cookies

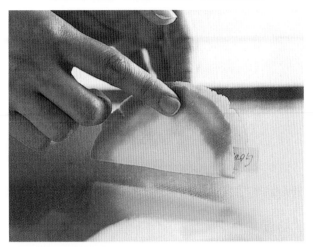

After placing a fortune across center of hot cookie, fold cookie in half and press edges together.

Immediately fold semicircle over edge of a small bowl to shape.

Clockwise from top:
Pennsylvania Dutch Brownies
(page 23), Almond Slices (page
193), Honey Cookies (opposite),
Christmas Rocks (page 215),
Pfeffernusse (page 137).

Honey Cookies

The recipe for these mildly honey-sweetened and slightly salty cookies was given to us by Dawn Zimmerman of Couderay, Wisconsin. She fondly remembers her Czechoslovakian grandma making them.

PREP: 40 MINUTES PLUS CHILLING   BAKE: 18 MINUTES PER BATCH
MAKES ABOUT 42 COOKIES

1 cup margarine or butter (2 sticks),   2 cups all-purpose flour
  softened   2 cups walnuts, chopped
1/4 cup honey   1/2 teaspoon salt
2 teaspoons vanilla extract

1. In large bowl, with mixer at high speed, beat margarine until creamy. Add honey and vanilla; beat until well blended. Reduce speed to low; beat in flour, walnuts, and salt until dough forms. Cover bowl with plastic wrap and refrigerate dough at least 1 hour.

2. Preheat oven to 325°F. With lightly floured hands, shape dough by heaping teaspoons into balls. Place balls, about 2 inches apart, on ungreased large cookie sheet. Press floured 4-tine fork across top of each ball.

3. Bake until golden, 18 to 22 minutes. With wide metal spatula, transfer cookies to wire rack to cool.

4. Repeat with remaining dough.

Each cookie: About 105 calories, 1 g protein, 7 g carbohydrate, 8 g total fat (1 g saturated), 0 mg cholesterol, 85 mg sodium.

Ladyfingers

Homemade ladyfingers are so delicious that it is hard to believe they are so easy to make. You can serve them alone or create old-fashioned desserts such as trifle.

PREP: 25 MINUTES   BAKE: 10 MINUTES

MAKES ABOUT 48 LADYFINGERS

4 large eggs, separated	1 teaspoon vanilla extract
1/8 teaspoon salt	3/4 cup all-purpose flour
3/4 cup granulated sugar	confectioners' sugar

1. Preheat oven to 350°F. Grease and flour two large cookie sheets.

2. In small bowl, with mixer at high speed, beat egg whites and salt until soft peaks form when beaters are lifted. Beating at high speed, gradually sprinkle in 1/4 cup granulated sugar, 1 tablespoon at a time, beating until sugar has dissolved and whites stand in stiff, glossy peaks when beaters are lifted.

3. In large bowl, with same beaters and with mixer at medium speed, beat egg yolks, remaining 1/2 cup granulated sugar, and vanilla until very thick and lemon-colored. With rubber spatula, fold in one-third of flour, then gently fold in remaining flour just until blended. Gently fold one-third of beaten egg whites into egg-yolk mixture. Fold in remaining egg whites just until blended.

4. Spoon half of batter into large pastry bag fitted with 1/2-inch plain tip. Pipe batter into 3-inch lengths, 1 inch apart, on prepared cookie sheets. If you like, with moistened finger, smooth edges. Lightly dust ladyfingers with confectioners' sugar. Repeat with remaining batter.

5. Bake until golden brown, 10 to 13 minutes, rotating cookie sheets between upper and lower oven racks halfway through baking. With wide metal spatula, transfer ladyfingers to wire racks to cool completely.

Each cookie: About 30 calories, 1 g protein, 5 g carbohydrate, 1 g total fat (0 g saturated), 18 mg cholesterol, 11 mg sodium.

Madeleines

The classic, shell-shaped, French sponge cakes extolled by Marcel Proust require a special pan for molding. But they taste so good you might want to consider buying your own madeleine pan. It makes a nice butter and candy mold as well.

PREP: 25 MINUTES   BAKE: 10 MINUTES PER BATCH
MAKES 24 MADELEINES

1 cup all-purpose flour
1/2 teaspoon baking powder
10 tablespoons butter (1 1/4 sticks), softened (do not use margarine)

3/4 cup sugar
3 large eggs
1 large egg yolk
1 1/2 teaspoons vanilla extract

1. Preheat oven to 400°F. Generously grease and flour madeleine pan. In small bowl, combine flour and baking powder.

2. In large bowl, with mixer at medium speed, beat butter and sugar until creamy, about 2 minutes. Add eggs, egg yolk, and vanilla. Increase speed to high and beat until pale yellow, about 3 minutes. Reduce speed to low and beat in flour mixture just until blended, scraping bowl with rubber spatula.

3. Spoon batter by rounded tablespoons into prepared pan. Bake until edges are browned and tops spring back when lightly pressed, 10 to 12 minutes. Let madeleines cool in pan 1 minute. With tip of table knife, release onto wire rack to cool completely.

4. Wash, grease, and flour pan. Repeat with remaining batter.

Each cookie: About 105 calories, 2 g protein, 11 g carbohydrate, 6 g total fat (3 g saturated), 48 mg cholesterol, 65 mg sodium.

Meringue Fingers

So much satisfaction for so few calories! The long, slow baking time at low temperature is essential to crisp the centers of the cookies without browning the outside.

PREP: 25 MINUTES PLUS COOLING   BAKE: 1 HOUR PER BATCH
MAKES ABOUT 48 COOKIES

3 large egg whites	1 teaspoon vanilla extract
1/4 teaspoon cream of tartar	2 squares (2 ounces) semisweet
1/8 teaspoon salt	chocolate
1/2 cup sugar	1 teaspoon vegetable shortening

1. Preheat oven to 200°F. Line two large cookie sheets with foil.

2. In medium bowl, with mixer at high speed, beat egg whites, cream of tartar, and salt until soft peaks form when beaters are lifted. Increase speed to high and gradually sprinkle in sugar, 2 tablespoons at a time, beating until sugar has dissolved. Add vanilla; continue beating until meringue stands in stiff, glossy peaks when beaters are lifted.

3. Spoon meringue into pastry bag fitted with 1/2-inch star tip. Pipe meringue into 3" by 1/2" fingers, about 1 inch apart, on prepared cookie sheets.

4. Bake until set, 1 hour, rotating sheets between upper and lower oven racks halfway through baking. Cool on cookie sheets on wire racks, 10 minutes. With small metal spatula, transfer cookies to wire racks to cool completely.

5. When cookies have cooled, in small saucepan, heat chocolate and shortening over low heat, stirring occasionally, until melted and smooth. Remove saucepan from heat. Dip one end of each cookie into melted chocolate mixture; let dry on wire racks over sheet of waxed paper.

Each cookie: About 15 calories, 0 g protein, 3 g carbohydrate, 0 g total fat, 0 mg cholesterol, 10 mg sodium.

Meringue Fingers

Mexican Wedding Cookies

Often called snowballs in America, these sugar-coated balls can also be made with almonds, walnuts, or toasted hazelnuts. In Mexico, where they originated, their name is *pastelitas de boda*. It is important to roll them in confectioners' sugar twice, once when slightly warm and again after they have cooled or immediately before serving.

PREP: 25 MINUTES   BAKE: 20 MINUTES PER BATCH
MAKES ABOUT 48 COOKIES

1 cup pecans
1 3/4 cups confectioners' sugar
1 cup butter (2 sticks), cut into
   16 pieces and softened (do not
   use margarine)

1 teaspoon vanilla extract
2 cups all-purpose flour

1. Preheat oven to 325°F.

2. In food processor with knife blade attached, process pecans and 1/4 cup sugar until nuts are finely chopped. Add butter and vanilla and process until smooth, scraping down sides of processor with rubber spatula. Add flour and process until combined and dough holds together.

3. With floured hands, shape dough by heaping teaspoons into 1-inch balls. Place balls 1 1/2 inches apart on ungreased large cookie sheet. Bake until bottoms are lightly browned and cookies are very light golden brown, 20 to 22 minutes. With wide metal spatula, transfer to wire rack to cool.

4. Place remaining 1 1/2 cups sugar in pie plate. While cookies are still warm, roll in sugar until coated and place on wire rack to cool completely. When cool, reroll cookies in sugar until thoroughly coated.

5. Repeat with remaining dough and sugar.

Each cookie: About 85 calories, 1 g protein, 9 g carbohydrate, 5 g total fat (3 g saturated), 10 mg cholesterol, 40 mg sodium.

Molasses Cookies

This recipe for an old-time favorite came from Amy Callaway, who remembers rolling the spicy dough into balls and dipping them in sugar when she was a child.

PREP: 40 MINUTES PLUS CHILLING   BAKE: 10 MINUTES PER BATCH
MAKES ABOUT 72 COOKIES

3/4 cup margarine or butter (1 1/2 sticks)	2 teaspoons baking soda
1/4 cup light (mild) molasses	1 teaspoon ground cinnamon
1 1/4 cups sugar	1/2 teaspoon ground ginger
1 large egg	1/2 teaspoon salt
2 cups all-purpose flour	1/4 teaspoon ground cloves

1. Preheat oven to 375°F. In 3-quart saucepan, melt margarine over low heat. Remove saucepan from heat and, with wire whisk, beat in molasses and 1 cup sugar until blended; whisk in egg. With wooden spoon, stir in flour, baking soda, cinnamon, ginger, salt, and cloves until mixed. Transfer dough to medium bowl and freeze until firm enough to handle, about 15 minutes.

2. Spread remaining 1/4 cup sugar on sheet of waxed paper. Roll dough into 1-inch balls; roll balls in sugar to coat. Place balls, 2 1/2 inches apart, on ungreased large cookie sheet.

3. Bake until cookies spread and darken, 10 to 12 minutes. Cool on cookie sheet on wire rack 1 minute, then transfer cookies to wire rack to cool completely.

4. Repeat with remaining dough.

Each cookie: About 45 calories, 1 g protein, 7 g carbohydrate, 2 g total fat (0 g saturated), 3 mg cholesterol, 75 mg sodium.

Noisettines

When Laurence Mancini Ilanjian was a student in Geneva, Switzerland, she loved the "noisettine" tarts at a local bakery. She developed these little hazelnut cookies—*noisette* means "hazelnut" in French—to re-create the flavor of the French delicacy.

PREP: 1 HOUR PLUS CHILLING   BAKE: 30 MINUTES
MAKES 24 COOKIES

1 package (3 ounces) cream cheese, softened
1/2 cup (1 stick) plus 1 tablespoon margarine or butter, softened
1 cup all-purpose flour
1 1/3 cups hazelnuts (filberts)
2/3 cup packed light brown sugar
1 large egg
1 teaspoon vanilla extract

1. In large bowl, with mixer at high speed, beat cream cheese and 1/2 cup margarine until creamy. Reduce speed to low; add flour and beat until well mixed. Cover bowl with plastic wrap and refrigerate 30 minutes.

2. Meanwhile, preheat oven to 350°F. Toast and skin hazelnuts (see page 73).

3. Reserve 24 hazelnuts for garnish. In food processor with knife blade attached, process remaining hazelnuts and brown sugar until hazelnuts are finely ground.

4. Prepare filling: In medium bowl, with spoon, combine hazelnut mixture, egg, vanilla, and remaining 1 tablespoon butter.

5. With floured hands, divide chilled dough into 24 equal pieces (dough will be very soft). Gently press each piece of dough evenly onto bottom and up sides of twenty-four 1 3/4" by 1" ungreased miniature muffin-pan cups. Spoon filling by heaping teaspoons into each pastry cup; place 1 whole hazelnut on top of filling in each cup.

6. Bake until filling is set and crust is golden, 30 minutes. With tip of knife, loosen cookie cups from muffin-pan cups and place on wire rack to cool completely.

Each cookie: About 135 calories, 2 g protein, 11 g carbohydrate, 10 g total fat (2 g saturated), 13 mg cholesterol, 75 mg sodium.

Pignoli Cookies

Thanks to the food processor—and prepared almond paste—making these pine nut–topped Italian cookies is a breeze. We use a pastry bag to form the rounds to keep our fingers from getting sticky.

Prep: 25 Minutes   Bake: 10 Minutes Per Batch
Makes About 24 Cookies

1 tube or can (7 to 8 ounces) almond paste	1 large egg white
	1 tablespoon plus 1 teaspoon honey
3/4 cup confectioners' sugar	1/2 cup pine nuts (pignoli)

1. Preheat oven to 350°F. Line two large cookie sheets with cooking parchment.

2. Crumble almond paste into food processor with knife blade attached. Add sugar and process until paste has texture of fine meal; transfer to large bowl. Add egg white and honey. With mixer at low speed, beat until blended. Increase speed to medium-high and beat until very smooth, 5 minutes.

3. Spoon batter into pastry bag fitted with 1/2-inch round tip. Pipe 1 1/4-inch rounds, 2 inches apart, on prepared cookie sheets. Brush cookies lightly with *water* and cover cookies completely with pine nuts, pressing nuts gently to stick.

4. Bake until golden brown, 10 to 12 minutes, rotating sheets between upper and lower oven racks halfway through baking. Slide parchment paper onto wire racks and let cookies cool on parchment paper.

5. Repeat with remaining dough and pine nuts.

Each cookie: About 75 calories, 2 g protein, 9 g carbohydrate, 4 g total fat (0 g saturated), 0 mg cholesterol, 5 mg sodium.

Pine-Nut Tassies

Folks will love these scrumptious tarts made with a cream-cheese crust and a toasted pine-nut and brown-sugar filling. Serve them for dessert or tea.

PREP: 40 MINUTES PLUS CHILLING   BAKE: 30 MINUTES

MAKES 24 COOKIES

1 cup pine nuts (pignoli)	1 cup all-purpose flour
1 package (3 ounces) cream cheese, softened	2 tablespoons granulated sugar
	2/3 cup packed light brown sugar
1/2 cup (1 stick) plus 1 tablespoon margarine or butter, softened	1 large egg
	1 teaspoon vanilla extract

1. Preheat oven to 350°F. Toast 3/4 cup pine nuts (see page 73). Cool completely.

2. Meanwhile, in large bowl, with mixer at high speed, beat cream cheese and 1/2 cup margarine until creamy. Reduce speed to low; add flour and granulated sugar and beat until well mixed. Cover bowl with plastic wrap; refrigerate 30 minutes.

3. Prepare filling: In food processor with knife blade attached, process toasted pine nuts and brown sugar until pine nuts are finely ground.

4. In medium bowl, with spoon, combine pine-nut mixture, egg, vanilla, and remaining 1 tablespoon butter.

5. With floured hands, divide chilled dough into 24 equal pieces (dough will be very soft). With floured fingertips, gently press each piece of dough evenly onto bottom and up sides of twenty-four 1 3/4" by 1" ungreased miniature muffin-pan cups. Spoon filling by heaping teaspoons into each pastry cup; sprinkle with remaining 1/4 cup pine nuts.

6. Bake until filling is set and crust is golden, 30 minutes. With tip of knife, loosen cookie cups from muffin-pan cups and place on wire rack to cool completely.

Each cookie: About 125 calories, 2 g protein, 12 g carbohydrate, 8 g total fat (2 g saturated), 13 mg cholesterol, 75 mg sodium.

Pretzel Cookies

With their golden-brown glaze and a sprinkling of coarse decorating sugar these pretty cookies look like salted pretzels. But one citrus-flavored bite reveals a scrumptious cookie.

PREP: 20 MINUTES   BAKE: 25 MINUTES
MAKES ABOUT 18 COOKIES

1/2 cup butter or margarine
   (1 stick), softened
1/3 cup granulated sugar
1 teaspoon freshly grated lemon or
   orange peel
1/4 teaspoon salt
1 large egg

2 large egg yolks
2 cups all-purpose flour
1/2 teaspoon water
coarse or granulated sugar for
   sprinkling
2 squares (2 ounces) semisweet
   chocolate, melted (optional)

1. Preheat oven to 350°F.
2. In large bowl, with mixer at medium speed, beat butter and granulated sugar until creamy. Add lemon or orange peel, salt, egg, and 1 egg yolk; beat until well blended. Reduce speed to low; add flour and beat until combined.
3. Gather dough into ball and knead on lightly floured surface. With hands, divide dough by heaping tablespoons into 20 pieces. Roll each piece into 11-inch-long rope. To shape each rope into a pretzel, form dough into an open loop then cross the ends and rest each one on bottom of loop. Place pretzels, 1 inch apart, on large ungreased cookie sheet.
4. In small cup, with fork, beat remaining egg yolk with water. Brush pretzels with glaze; sprinkle with coarse sugar. Bake until golden brown, 25 to 28 minutes. Cool on cookie sheet on wire rack 3 minutes. With wide metal spatula, transfer cookies to wire rack to cool completely. When cool, drizzle melted chocolate over cookies, if you like; let chocolate set before serving.

Each cookie without chocolate: About 115 calories, 2 g protein, 15 g carbohydrate, 5 g total fat (3 g saturated), 44 mg cholesterol, 80 mg sodium.

Raspberry Linzer Cookies

Raspberry Linzer Cookies

Our hazelnut cookies topped with raspberry jam deliver all the flavor of the traditional Austrian linzertorte without the fuss.

PREP: 45 MINUTES   BAKE: 20 MINUTES PER BATCH
MAKES ABOUT 48 COOKIES

1 1/3 cups hazelnuts (filberts)
1/2 cup sugar
3/4 cup butter or margarine (1 1/2 sticks), cut into pieces

1 teaspoon vanilla extract
1/4 teaspoon salt
1 3/4 cups all-purpose flour
1/4 cup seedless red-raspberry jam

1. Preheat oven to 350°F. Toast and skin 1 cup hazelnuts (see page 73); set aside remaining 1/3 cup.

2. In food processor with knife blade attached, process 1 cup toasted hazelnuts and sugar until nuts are finely ground. Add butter, vanilla, and salt and process until blended. Add flour and process until evenly combined. Remove knife blade and press dough together with hands.

3. Finely chop remaining 1/3 cup hazelnuts; spread on sheet of waxed paper. With hands shape dough, 2 teaspoons at a time, into 1-inch balls (dough may be slightly crumbly). Roll balls in nuts, gently pressing nuts into dough. Place balls, about 1 1/2 inches apart, on ungreased large cookie sheet.

4. With tip of spoon, make small indentation in center of each ball. Fill each indentation with 1/4 teaspoon jam. Bake until lightly golden around edges, 20 minutes. With wide metal spatula, transfer cookies to wire racks to cool completely.

5. Repeat with remaining balls and jam.

Each cookie: About 75 calories, 1 g protein, 7 g carbohydrate, 5 g total fat (2 g saturated), 8 mg cholesterol, 40 mg sodium.

Snickerdoodles

Despite their funny name, these cinnamon sugar–coated butter cookies became a favorite all across the country and are now considered an American classic. They are so much fun to make, the kids will beg to help.

PREP: 25 MINUTES   BAKE: 12 MINUTES PER BATCH

MAKES ABOUT 54 COOKIES

3 cups all-purpose flour	1 1/3 cups plus 1/4 cup sugar
2 teaspoons cream of tartar	2 large eggs
1 teaspoon baking soda	1 teaspoon vanilla extract
1 cup butter or margarine (2 sticks), softened	1 1/2 teaspoons ground cinnamon

1. Preheat oven to 375°F. In large bowl, stir together flour, cream of tartar, and baking soda.

2. In separate large bowl, with mixer at medium speed, beat butter and 1 1/3 cups sugar until light and fluffy. Beat in eggs and vanilla. Reduce speed to low; beat in flour mixture until well blended.

3. In small bowl, combine cinnamon and remaining 1/4 cup sugar. With hands, shape dough into 1-inch balls. Roll in cinnamon-sugar to coat. Place balls, 1 inch apart, on ungreased large cookie sheet. Bake until set and lightly golden and slightly crinkly on top, 12 minutes. Cool on cookie sheet on wire rack 1 minute. With wide metal spatula, transfer cookies to wire racks to cool completely.

4. Repeat with remaining dough.

Each cookie: About 80 calories, 1 g protein, 11 g carbohydrate, 4 g total fat (2 g saturated), 17 mg cholesterol, 60 mg sodium.

Thumbprint Cookies

Alice Garbarini Hurley was given this recipe by her mother-in-law, who lives in Bangor, Maine, where the favorite jam is usually homemade blueberry. Raspberry or strawberry would also be good.

PREP: 40 MINUTES   BAKE: 20 MINUTES PER BATCH
MAKES 56 COOKIES

2 large eggs	1/2 teaspoon almond extract
3/4 cup margarine or butter	1/4 teaspoon salt
(1 1/2 sticks), softened	2 cups all-purpose flour
3/4 cup sugar	1 1/4 cups walnuts, finely chopped
1/2 teaspoon vanilla extract	1/2 cup favorite jam

1. Preheat oven to 350°F. Grease large cookie sheet.

2. In large bowl, with fork, beat eggs lightly. Measure out 3 tablespoons beaten egg and transfer to small bowl for later use.

3. Add margarine, sugar, vanilla and almond extracts, and salt to eggs in large bowl. With mixer at medium speed, beat until evenly mixed, occasionally scraping bowl with rubber spatula. Add flour and stir just until blended.

4. Divide dough into 4 equal pieces. Divide each piece into 14 pieces and shape into balls. Spread walnuts on a sheet of waxed paper. Dip balls in reserved egg, then roll in walnuts, gently pressing nuts into dough.

5. Place balls, 2 inches apart, on prepared cookie sheet. With thumb, make small indentation in center of each ball. Bake until golden, 20 minutes. Transfer cookies to wire rack. Immediately fill each indentation with a rounded 1/4 teaspoon of jam. Cool cookies completely on wire rack.

6. Repeat with remaining balls and jam.

Each cookie: About 90 calories, 1 g protein, 10 g carbohydrate, 5 g total fat (1 g saturated), 9 mg cholesterol, 55 mg sodium.

Tulipes

Place a scoop of ice cream, fresh fruit, or both in these versatile free-form tart shells and you'll have a memorable dessert. They can be made up to a week ahead.

PREP: 30 MINUTES PLUS COOLING   BAKE: 5 MINUTES PER BATCH
MAKES ABOUT 12 TULIPES

3 large egg whites	1/2 teaspoon vanilla extract
3/4 cup confectioners' sugar	1/4 teaspoon salt
1/2 cup all-purpose flour	1 quart ice cream or sorbet
6 tablespoons butter (3/4 stick), melted (do not use margarine)	

1. Preheat oven to 350°F. Grease large cookie sheet.

2. In large bowl, with wire whisk, beat egg whites, sugar, and flour until blended and smooth. Beat in melted butter, vanilla, and salt.

3. Drop 1 heaping tablespoon batter on prepared cookie sheet. With small metal spatula or back of spoon, spread in circular motion to form 4-inch round. Repeat to make 2 cookies, placing them 4 inches apart. Bake until edges are golden, 5 to 7 minutes.

4. Place two 2-inch-diameter glasses upside down on surface. With wide metal spatula, quickly lift 1 hot cookie and gently shape over bottom of glass. Shape second cookie. When cookies are cool, transfer to wire rack. If cookies become too firm to shape, return cookie sheet to oven to soften cookies slightly.

5. Repeat Steps 3 and 4 with remaining batter. (Batter will become slightly thicker upon standing.) To serve, place on dessert plates and fill each with a scoop of ice cream.

Each serving with ice cream: About 190 calories, 3 g protein, 22 g carbohydrate, 11 g total fat (7 g saturated), 35 mg cholesterol, 155 mg sodium.

Tulipes

Sicilian Sesame Cookies

Here are cookies you can serve as a snack any time of day, even early morning, because they're not too sweet. To coat the dough quickly, put the toasted sesame seeds in a small plastic bag, add the logs of dough one at a time, and shake gently.

PREP: 30 MINUTES   BAKE: 30 MINUTES PER BATCH
MAKES 48 COOKIES

1 cup sesame seeds	1/4 teaspoon salt
(about 5 ounces)	3 large eggs, beaten
2 1/4 cups all-purpose flour	4 tablespoons butter or margarine
3/4 cup sugar	(1/2 stick), melted
2 teaspoons baking powder	1 teaspoon vanilla extract

1. Preheat oven to 350°F. Spread sesame seeds in single layer on jelly-roll pan; bake, stirring once, until golden, 8 to 10 minutes. Cool on wire rack, then transfer to small bowl.

2. In large bowl, stir together flour, sugar, baking powder, and salt. In small bowl, stir together eggs, melted butter, and vanilla. Add egg mixture to flour mixture, stirring just until blended.

3. Transfer dough to lightly floured surface. With hands, knead dough five or six times until smooth. Divide dough into quarters. Roll 1 piece into a 24-inch-long rope; with knife, cut crosswise into twelve 2-inch logs.

4. Fill small bowl with *water*. Dip each log in the water and roll in the toasted sesame seeds until completely coated. Place logs, 1 inch apart, on two ungreased large cookie sheets. Bake until golden brown, 30 to 35 minutes, rotating sheets between upper and lower racks halfway through baking. With wide metal spatula, transfer cookies to wire racks to cool completely. (Cookies will firm up as they cool.)

5. Repeat with remaining dough and sesame seeds.

Each cookie: About 65 calories, 2 g protein, 9 g carbohydrate, 3 g total fat (1 g saturated), 16 mg cholesterol, 45 mg sodium.

Chocolate Chip Biscotti

The crispy low-fat Italian cookies called biscotti took America by storm in the late 1980s. Originally served with coffee or after-dinner liqueurs, they now appear in lunch boxes, cookie jars, and bake sales.

PREP: 45 MINUTES PLUS COOLING   BAKE: 40 MINUTES
MAKES ABOUT 60 COOKIES

2 cups all-purpose flour
1 cup sugar
1 teaspoon baking powder
1/4 teaspoon salt
pinch ground cinnamon
4 tablespoons cold margarine or
  butter (1/2 stick), cut into pieces

3 large eggs, lightly beaten
1 package (6 ounces) semisweet
  chocolate mini chips (1 cup)
1 cup walnuts, toasted (see page 73)
  and coarsely chopped
1 teaspoon vanilla extract

1. Preheat oven to 350°F. In large bowl, mix flour, sugar, baking powder, salt, and cinnamon. With pastry blender or two knives used scissor-fashion, cut in margarine until mixture resembles fine crumbs.

2. Spoon 1 tablespoon beaten eggs into cup; reserve. Add chocolate chips, walnuts, vanilla, and remaining beaten eggs to flour mixture; stir until evenly moistened. With hand, knead mixture a few times in bowl until dough forms.

3. On floured surface, with floured hands, divide dough into quarters. Shape each quarter into 9" by 2" log. Place logs crosswise, 4 inches apart, on two large ungreased cookie sheets. With pastry brush, brush tops and sides of logs with reserved egg. Bake until lightly browned, 25 minutes. Cool logs on cookie sheet on wire rack 10 minutes.

4. Transfer 1 log to cutting board. With serrated knife, cut warm log cross-wise on diagonal into 1/2-inch-thick slices. Place slices upright, 1/4 inch apart, on same cookie sheets. Repeat with remaining logs. Return to oven and bake 15 minutes to dry biscotti. Cool completely on cookie sheets on wire racks. (Biscotti will harden as they cool.)

Each cookie: About 65 calories, 1 g protein, 9 g carbohydrate, 3 g total fat (0 g saturated), 1 mg cholesterol, 30 mg sodium.

Almond-Anise Biscotti

Soaking the anise seeds in liqueur softens them and releases their delicious flavor.

PREP: 25 MINUTES PLUS COOLING   BAKE: 55 MINUTES
MAKES ABOUT 120 COOKIES

1 tablespoon anise seeds, crushed	1 cup whole almonds (4 ounces), toasted (see page 73) and coarsely chopped
1 tablespoon anise-flavored aperitif or liqueur	1 teaspoon baking powder
2 cups all-purpose flour	1/8 teaspoon salt
1 cup sugar	3 large eggs

1. Preheat oven to 325°F. In medium bowl, combine anise seeds and anise-flavored aperitif; let stand 10 minutes.

2. Grease large cookie sheet. In large bowl, combine flour, sugar, chopped almonds, baking powder, and salt. With wire whisk, beat eggs into anise mixture. With wooden spoon, stir egg mixture into flour mixture until blended.

3. Divide dough in half. On prepared cookie sheet, with floured hands, shape each half into 15-inch log, placing them 3 inches apart (dough will be sticky). Bake until golden and toothpick inserted in center comes out clean, about 40 minutes. Cool on cookie sheet on wire rack, 10 minutes.

4. Transfer logs to cutting board. With serrated knife, cut each log cross-wise on diagonal into 1/4-inch-thick slices. Place slices, cut side down, on two ungreased cookie sheets. Bake 15 minutes, turning slices over once and rotating cookie sheets between upper and lower oven racks halfway through baking. With wide metal spatula, transfer biscotti to wire racks to cool completely.

Each cookie: About 23 calories, 1 g protein, 4 g carbohydrate, 1 g total fat (0 g saturated), 6 mg cholesterol, 8 mg sodium.

Chocolate-Brownie Biscotti

Enjoy rich brownie flavor, Italian style! Patricia Ambrosini's family has myriad uses for these crisp chocolate cookies. We think yours will too.

PREP: 45 MINUTES PLUS COOLING   BAKE: 50 MINUTES
MAKES ABOUT 48 COOKIES

2 1/2 cups all-purpose flour
1 1/3 cups sugar
3/4 cup unsweetened cocoa
2 teaspoons baking powder
1/2 teaspoon baking soda
1/2 teaspoon salt
1/2 cup butter or margarine
  (1 stick), melted

3 large eggs
2 teaspoons vanilla extract
1 cup almonds, toasted (see page
  73) and coarsely chopped
4 squares (4 ounces) semisweet
  chocholate, coarsely chopped

1. Preheat oven to 325°F. In medium bowl, mix flour, sugar, cocoa, baking powder, baking soda, and salt.
2. In large bowl, with mixer at medium speed, beat butter, eggs, and vanilla until mixed. Reduce speed to low; gradually add flour mixture and beat just until blended. With hand, knead in almonds and chocolate until combined.
3. Divide dough in half. On ungreased large cookie sheet, shape each half into 12" by 3" log, placing them about 3 inches apart. Bake until lightly browned, 30 minutes. Cool logs on cookie sheet on wire rack 15 minutes.
4. Transfer logs to cutting board. With serrated knife, cut each log crosswise on diagonal into 1/2-inch-thick slices. Place slices upright, 1/4 inch apart, on same cookie sheet. Return to oven and bake 20 minutes to dry biscotti. Cool completely on cookie sheet on wire rack. (Biscotti will harden as they cool.)

Each cookie: about 101 calories, 2 g protein, 13 g carbohydrate, 5 g total fat (2 g saturated), 19 mg cholesterol, 79 mg sodium.

Chocolate–Dried Cherry Biscotti

For a tasty all-American twist, we added dried tart cherries to the original Italian twice-baked chocolate cookie.

PREP: 30 MINUTES PLUS COOLING   BAKE: 45 MINUTES
MAKES ABOUT 48 COOKIES

1 teaspoon instant espresso-coffee powder
1 teaspoon hot water
2 1/2 cups all-purpose flour
3/4 cup unsweetened cocoa
1 tablespoon baking powder
1/2 teaspoon salt
2 squares (2 ounces) semisweet chocolate, chopped

1/2 cup butter or margarine (1 stick), softened
1 1/3 cups sugar
3 large eggs
3/4 cup dried tart cherries, coarsely chopped

1. Preheat oven to 350°F. Grease and flour large cookie sheet. In cup, dissolve espresso powder in hot water; set aside.

2. In medium bowl, combine flour, cocoa, baking powder, and salt. In heavy 1-quart saucepan, melt chocolate over low heat, stirring frequently, until smooth. Remove pan from heat; cool.

3. In large bowl, with mixer at medium speed, beat butter and sugar until light and fluffy. Reduce speed to low; add eggs, one at a time, and beat until blended. Add cooled chocolate and espresso; beat until blended. Add flour mixture and beat just until blended. With hand, knead in cherries.

4. With floured hands, divide dough in half. On ungreased large cookie sheet, shape each half into 12" by 3" loaf, placing them about 3 inches apart. With pastry brush, brush off any excess flour. Bake until lightly browned, 30 minutes. Cool on cookie sheet on wire rack 10 minutes.

5. Transfer loaves to cutting board. With serrated knife, cut each loaf crosswise on diagonal into 1/2-inch-thick slices. Place slices, cut side down, on same cookie sheet. Return to oven and bake 15 to 20 minutes to dry biscotti. With wide metal spatula, transfer biscotti to wire racks to cool completely. (Biscotti will harden as they cool.)

Each cookie: About 83 calories, 1 g protein, 14 g carbohydrate, 3 g total fat (2 g saturated), 17 mg cholesterol, 79 mg sodium.

Greek Cinnamon Paximadia

Here's a Greek version of biscotti (*paximadia* is Greek for "biscuits") sent to us by Kathryn Marie Petrofanis of San Pedro, California.

PREP: 1 HOUR PLUS COOLING   BAKE: 50 MINUTES
MAKES ABOUT 64 COOKIES

1/2 cup margarine or butter (1 stick), softened	1 teaspoon vanilla extract
1/2 cup vegetable shortening	4 to 4 1/2 cups all-purpose flour
1 1/2 cups sugar	2 teaspoons baking powder
3 large eggs	1/2 teaspoon baking soda
	1 1/2 teaspoons ground cinnamon

1. In large bowl, with mixer at low speed, beat margarine, shortening, and 1 cup sugar until blended. Increase speed to high; beat until light and fluffy, about 5 minutes. At low speed, add eggs, one at a time, and vanilla; beat until well mixed.

2. Gradually add 3 cups flour, baking powder, and baking soda; beat until well blended. With wooden spoon, stir in 1 cup flour until soft dough forms. If necessary, add additional flour (up to 1/2 cup) until dough is easy to handle.

3. Preheat oven to 350°F. Divide dough into 4 equal pieces. On lightly floured surface, shape each piece of dough into 8-inch-long log. Place 2 logs, about 4 inches apart, on each of two ungreased large cookie sheets. Flatten each log to 2 1/2 inches wide.

4. Bake until lightly browned and toothpick inserted in center comes out clean, 20 minutes, rotating cookie sheets between upper and lower oven racks halfway through baking. In pie plate, mix remaining 1/2 cup sugar and cinnamon.

5. Transfer hot loaves (during baking, logs will spread and become loaves) to cutting board. With serrated knife, cut crosswise on diagonal into 1/2-inch-thick slices. Coat slices with cinnamon-sugar. Return slices, cut side down, to same cookie sheets. Bake 15 minutes. Turn slices over and return to oven; bake until golden, 15 minutes longer, rotating cookie sheets between upper and lower racks. Transfer cookies to wire racks to cool.

Each cookie: About 79 calories, 1 g protein, 11 g carbohydrate, 4 g total fat (1 g saturated), 10 mg cholesterol, 45 mg sodium.

Mandelbrot

An Eastern European cookie, mandelbrot, or almond bread, is baked in logs, sliced, and rebaked just like biscotti. There are many variations on the classic recipe: some feature nuts; others dried fruit, chocolate pieces, or a swirl of cocoa.

PREP: 30 MINUTES PLUS COOLING   BAKE: 37 MINUTES
MAKES ABOUT 48 COOKIES

3 3/4 cups all-purpose flour
2 teaspoons baking powder
1/2 teaspoon salt
3 large eggs
1 cup sugar
3/4 cup vegetable oil
2 teaspoons vanilla extract

1/4 teaspoon almond extract
1 teaspoon freshly grated orange peel
1 cup blanched almonds, coarsely chopped and toasted (see page 73) until golden

1. Preheat oven to 350°F. In large bowl, stir together flour, baking powder, and salt.

2. In separate large bowl, with mixer at medium speed, beat eggs and sugar until light lemon-colored. Add oil, vanilla and almond extracts, and orange peel and beat until blended. With wooden spoon, beat in flour mixture until combined. Stir in almonds.

3. Divide dough in half. Drop each half by spoonfuls down length of ungreased large cookie sheet. With lightly floured hands, shape each half into 12-inch-long log, leaving 4 inches between logs (dough will be slightly sticky). Bake until lightly colored and firm, 30 minutes. Cool on cookie sheet on wire rack 10 minutes.

4. Transfer logs to cutting board. With serrated knife, cut each log crosswise into 1/2-inch-thick slices. Place slices, cut side down, on two ungreased cookie sheets. Bake until golden, 7 to 8 minutes, turning slices over and rotating sheets between upper and lower racks halfway through baking. With wide metal spatula, transfer cookies to wire racks to cool completely.

Each cookie: About 105 calories, 2 g protein, 12 g carbohydrate, 5 g total fat (1 g saturated), 13 mg cholesterol, 50 mg sodium.

Mandelbrot

Ginger Biscotti

Small chunks of crystallized ginger give these crisp cookies a piquant bite. Be sure to cool them completely, then pack into a tight jar to keep them crisp.

PREP: 25 MINUTES PLUS COOLING   BAKE: 48 MINUTES
MAKES ABOUT 48 COOKIES

3 cups all-purpose flour
1 tablespoon ground ginger
2 teaspoons baking powder
1/4 teaspoon salt
1/2 cup butter or margarine
  (1 stick), softened

1/2 cup granulated sugar
1/2 cup packed light brown sugar
3 large eggs
1/2 cup finely chopped crystallized
  ginger

1. Preheat oven to 350°F. Grease large cookie sheet. In medium bowl, stir together flour, ground ginger, baking powder, and salt.

2. In large bowl, with mixer at medium speed, beat butter and granulated and brown sugars until light and creamy. Beat in eggs, one at a time. Reduce speed to low and beat in flour mixture until combined; stir in crystallized ginger.

3. Divide dough in half; drop each half by spoonfuls down length of prepared cookie sheet. With floured hands, shape each half into 12-inch-long log, leaving about 3 inches between logs. Bake until toothpick inserted in center of logs comes out clean, 30 minutes. Cool logs on cookie sheet on wire rack 10 minutes.

4. Transfer logs to cutting board. With serrated knife, cut each log crosswise on diagonal into 1/2-inch-thick slices. Place slices, cut side down, on two ungreased cookie sheets. Bake until golden, 20 minutes, turning slices over and rotating sheets between upper and lower racks halfway through baking, until golden. With wide metal spatula, transfer biscotti to wire racks to cool completely.

Each cookie: About 90 calories, 1 g protein, 15 g carbohydrate, 3 g total fat (2 g saturated), 21 mg cholesterol, 65 mg sodium.

Almond Slices

Ann Woods's grandmother baked and sold these crisp, thin cookies in Greensboro, North Carolina, during the 1930s.

PREP: 45 MINUTES PLUS FREEZING   BAKE: 15 MINUTES PER BATCH
MAKES ABOUT 256 COOKIES

1 1/2 cups butter (3 sticks), melted (do not use margarine)
1 cup packed light brown sugar
1 cup granulated sugar
3 large eggs
1 teaspoon vanilla extract
1/2 teaspoon lemon extract

1 cup slivered blanched almonds, finely ground
5 1/2 cups all-purpose flour
2 teaspoons ground cinnamon
1 1/2 teaspoons baking soda
1 teaspoon ground nutmeg
1 teaspoon salt

1. In large bowl, with spoon, combine melted butter and brown and granulated sugars. Add eggs, vanilla and lemon extracts, and ground almonds; beat until well combined. Stir in flour, cinnamon, baking soda, nutmeg, and salt until dough forms. Cover bowl with plastic wrap and freeze dough until easy to handle, 1 hour.

2. Divide dough into 8 pieces. On lightly floured surface, with floured hands, shape each piece into 6-inch-long log. Wrap each log in plastic and freeze until firm enough to slice, at least 4 hours or overnight.

3. Preheat oven to 350°F. Grease two large cookie sheets. Slice 1 log into very thin (about 3/16-inch-thick) slices; keep remaining dough refrigerated. Place slices, 1 1/2 inches apart, on prepared cookie sheets. Bake until browned, 15 minutes, rotating sheets between upper and lower oven racks halfway through baking. With wide metal spatula, transfer cookies to wire rack to cool.

4. Repeat with remaining dough.

Each cookie: About 25 calories, 0 g protein, 3 g carbohydrate, 1 g total fat (0 g saturated), 5 mg cholesterol, 25 mg sodium.

Anise Slices

These aromatic cookies are perfect with a cup of tea or coffee. If you don't have a mortar and pestle to crush the anise seeds, you can coarsely grind them in a spice grinder. Or place them in a plastic bag and crush them with a rolling pin.

PREP: 30 MINUTES PLUS CHILLING BAKE: 12 MINUTES PER BATCH
MAKES ABOUT 88 COOKIES

1/2 cup butter (1 stick), softened
  (do not use margarine)
3/4 cup sugar
1 large egg
1/2 teaspoon vanilla extract

1 3/4 cups all-purpose flour
1 tablespoon anise seeds, crushed
1/2 teaspoon baking powder
1/4 teaspoon salt

1. In large bowl, with mixer at medium speed, beat butter and sugar until creamy, about 1 minute, occasionally scraping bowl with rubber spatula. Reduce speed to low; beat in egg and vanilla until blended. Beat in flour, anise seeds, baking powder, and salt until well combined, occasionally scraping bowl.

2. Divide dough in half. Shape each half into 5 1/2" by 2" rectangle. Wrap each rectangle in plastic wrap and refrigerate until dough is firm enough to slice, 2 hours. (Or freeze dough for 1 hour.)

3. Preheat oven to 350°F. Grease large cookie sheet. With knife, cut 1 rectangle crosswise into scant 1/8-inch-thick slices; keep remaining dough refrigerated. Place cookies, 1 inch apart, on prepared cookie sheet. Bake cookies until lightly browned, 12 to 14 minutes. With wide metal spatula, transfer cookies to wire rack to cool.

4. Repeat with remaining dough.

Each cookie: About 25 calories, 0 g protein, 3 g carbohydrate, 2 g total fat (1 g saturated), 6 mg cholesterol, 21 mg sodium.

Cinnamon Spirals

A spiral of aromatic spice runs through a cream-cheese dough. The result is a delicious contrast of colors and flavors.

PREP: 40 MINUTES PLUS CHILLING   BAKE: 12 MINUTES PER BATCH
MAKES ABOUT 60 COOKIES

1/2 cup butter or margarine
  (1 stick), softened
4 ounces cream cheese, softened
1 1/4 cups all-purpose flour

1/4 teaspoon salt
1/3 cup sugar
1 teaspoon ground cinnamon

1. In large bowl, with mixer at medium speed, beat butter and cream cheese until creamy, about 2 minutes. Reduce speed to low; gradually beat in flour and salt until well mixed, occasionally scraping bowl with rubber spatula.

2. On sheet of plastic wrap, pat dough into small rectangle. Wrap dough in plastic and refrigerate until dough is firm enough to roll, 1 hour. (Or freeze dough for 30 minutes.)

3. Meanwhile, in small bowl, mix sugar and cinnamon; set aside.

4. On lightly floured surface, with floured rolling pin, roll cookie dough into 15" by 12" rectangle. Sprinkle cinnamon-sugar mixture evenly over dough. Starting from one long side, tightly roll rectangle jelly-roll fashion. Brush last 1/2 inch of dough with water to help seal edge. Cut log crosswise in half. Slide logs onto ungreased cookie sheet; cover with plastic wrap and refrigerate until dough is firm enough to slice, 2 hours. (Or freeze dough for 45 minutes.)

5. Preheat oven to 400°F. Remove 1 log from refrigerator or freezer. With serrated knife, cut log crosswise into 1/4-inch-thick slices. Place slices, 1/2 inch apart, on ungreased large cookie sheet. Bake until lightly browned, 12 to 14 minutes. With wide metal spatula, transfer cookies to wire rack to cool.

6. Repeat with remaining dough.

Each cookie: About 36 calories, 1 g protein, 3 g carbohydrate, 2 g total fat (2 g saturated), 6 mg cholesterol, 32 mg sodium.

Checkerboard Cookies

Chocolate and vanilla make up the tasty checkerboard design of these refrigerator squares. The secret to getting the two doughs not to break apart after baking is to brush all the adjoining areas with milk before chilling.

PREP: 40 MINUTES PLUS CHILLING   BAKE: 10 MINUTES PER BATCH
MAKES ABOUT 48 COOKIES

2 cups all-purpose flour	1 large egg
1 teaspoon baking powder	1 teaspoon vanilla extract
1/4 teaspoon salt	1 square (1 ounce) semisweet
1/2 cup (1 stick) plus 1 tablespoon	chocolate
butter or margarine, softened	3 tablespoons unsweetened cocoa
1 cup sugar	milk for assembling cookies

1. In medium bowl, combine flour, baking powder, and salt. In medium bowl, with mixer at medium speed, beat 1/2 cup butter and sugar until creamy. Reduce speed to low and beat in egg and vanilla until blended. Beat in flour mixture until combined, scraping bowl occasionally with rubber spatula. Remove half of dough; set aside.

2. In 1-quart saucepan, melt chocolate and remaining 1 tablespoon butter over very low heat. Stir in cocoa until combined. Add chocolate mixture to dough in bowl, stirring until blended.

3. Separately shape chocolate and vanilla doughs into 12" by 2" by 1" blocks. Slice each block lengthwise into two 12" by 1" by 1" strips. Brush one side of 1 chocolate strip with milk; place brushed side next to 1 vanilla strip. Repeat with remaining 2 strips. Brush top of one of the vanilla/chocolate rectangles with milk. Place second vanilla/chocolate rectangle on top, reversing colors so end forms checkerboard. Wrap block in waxed paper, using paper to square edges. Refrigerate 4 hours or overnight. (If using margarine, freeze overnight.)

4. Preheat oven to 375°F. Grease two large cookie sheets. Cut dough into 1/4-inch-thick slices. Place slices, 1/2-inch apart, on prepared cookie sheets. Bake until golden, 10 to 12 minutes. Cool on cookie sheets on wire racks 5 minutes. With wide metal spatula, transfer to wire racks to cool completely.

Each cookie: About 62 calories, 1 g protein, 9 g carbohydrate, 2 g total fat (1 g saturated), 10 mg cholesterol, 45 mg sodium.

FORMING AND SLICING CHECKERBOARD DOUGH

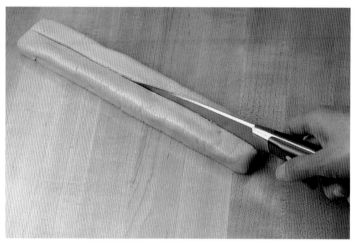

Cut each 12" by 2" by 1" block of dough in half lengthwise to make two strips.

After dough has been assembled and chilled, slice it into 1/4-inch-thick checkerboard cookies.

Coconut Thins

Flecks of toasted coconut make a pretty pattern on wafer-thin cookies. It is essential that the dough be very cold and firm, or it will be difficult to cut thinly.

PREP: 30 MINUTES PLUS CHILLING   BAKE: 8 MINUTES PER BATCH
MAKES ABOUT 112 COOKIES

2 cups (6 ounces) flaked sweetened coconut
1 3/4 cups all-purpose flour
1/4 cup cornstarch
1/2 teaspoon baking powder
1/8 teaspoon ground nutmeg
1/8 teaspoon salt

3/4 cup butter or margarine (1 1/2 sticks), softened
1 cup sugar
1 large egg
1/2 teaspoon vanilla extract
1/4 teaspoon almond extract

1. Preheat oven to 350°F. In jelly-roll pan, toast coconut, stirring occasionally, until lightly golden, 9 to 10 minutes. In large bowl, stir together toasted coconut, flour, cornstarch, baking powder, nutmeg, and salt.

2. In separate large bowl, with mixer at medium speed, beat butter and sugar until light and fluffy. Beat in egg and vanilla and almond extracts until well combined. Reduce speed to low and beat in flour mixture until well combined.

3. Divide dough in half. On separate sheets of waxed paper, shape each half into 14" by 1 1/2" log. Wrap each log in the waxed paper, rolling it up tightly. Refrigerate several hours, until very firm; or label, date, and freeze.

4. Preheat oven to 350°F. Cut 1 log crosswise into 1/4-inch-thick slices; keep remaining dough refrigerated. Place slices, 1 inch apart, on two ungreased large cookie sheets. Bake until edges are golden brown, 8 to 9 minutes, rotating sheets between upper and lower racks halfway through baking. Cool on cookie sheets on wire rack 1 minute. With wide metal spatula, transfer to wire racks to cool completely.

5. Repeat with remaining dough.

Each cookie: About 32 calories, 0 g protein, 4 g carbohydrate, 2 g total fat (1 g saturated), 5 mg cholesterol, 21 mg sodium.

Garden-Party Sugar Cookies

Fresh thyme, lemon peel, and crystallized ginger bring complex flavor to these easy-to-make cookies. They're perfect with iced tea or lemonade.

PREP: 30 MINUTES PLUS CHILLING AND COOLING
BAKE: 12 MINUTES PER BATCH
MAKES ABOUT 96 COOKIES

2 1/2 cups all-purpose flour
1 teaspoon baking soda
1 teaspoon cream of tartar
1/2 teaspoon salt
1 cup margarine or butter (2 sticks), softened
2 cups confectioners' sugar

1 large egg
1 tablespoon freshly grated lemon peel
1 tablespoon fresh thyme leaves (preferably lemon thyme), minced
1 tablespoon minced crystallized ginger

1. In medium bowl, combine flour, baking soda, cream of tartar, and salt.

2. In large bowl, with mixer at low speed, beat margarine and confectioners' sugar until blended. Increase speed to high; beat until creamy. Reduce speed to low; beat in egg, lemon peel, thyme, and ginger. Beat in flour mixture just until blended.

3. Divide dough in half. Shape each half into 12" by 1 1/2" squared-off log; wrap each log in plastic. Freeze until firm enough to slice, 2 hours. (Logs can be frozen up to 1 month.)

4. Preheat oven to 350°F. Cut 1 log crosswise into 1/4-inch-thick slices. Place slices, 1 inch apart, on ungreased large cookie sheet. Bake until edges are golden brown, 12 to 14 minutes. With wide metal spatula, transfer to wire rack to cool.

5. Repeat with remaining dough.

Each cookie: About 40 calories, 0 g protein, 5 g carbohydrate, 2 g total fat (0 g saturated), 2 mg cholesterol, 50 mg sodium.

Lemon Slices

The silky, melt-in-your-mouth texture of these thinly sliced lemon cookies comes from confectioners' sugar. For a special treat, sandwich them with lemon frosting or bittersweet chocolate.

PREP: 30 MINUTES PLUS CHILLING
BAKE: 12 MINUTES PER BATCH
MAKES ABOUT 48 COOKIES

2 cups all-purpose flour	1/2 cup plus 2 tablespoons
1/4 teaspoon baking powder	granulated sugar
1/4 teaspoon salt	1/2 cup confectioners' sugar
2 to 3 large lemons	1/2 teaspoon vanilla extract
3/4 cup butter or margarine (1 1/2 sticks), softened	

1. In medium bowl, stir together flour, baking powder, and salt. From lemons, grate 1 tablespoon peel and squeeze 2 tablespoons juice.

2. In large bowl, with mixer at medium speed, beat butter, 1/2 cup granulated sugar, and confectioners' sugar until creamy. Beat in lemon peel and juice and vanilla until blended. Reduce speed to low and beat in flour mixture just until combined.

3. Divide dough in half. Shape each half into 6-inch-long log. Wrap each log in waxed paper and refrigerate overnight. (If using margarine, freeze overnight.)

4. Preheat oven to 350°F. Cut 1 log crosswise into scant 1/4-inch-thick slices; keep remaining log refrigerated. Place slices, 1 1/2 inches apart, on ungreased large cookie sheet. Sprinkle slices lightly with some of remaining 2 tablespoons granulated sugar. Bake until edges are lightly browned, 12 minutes. Cool on cookie sheet on wire rack 2 minutes. With wide metal spatula, transfer to wire racks to cool completely.

5. Repeat with remaining dough and granulated sugar.

Each cookie: About 63 calories, 1 g protein, 8 g carbohydrate, 3 g total fat (1 g saturated), 8 mg cholesterol, 44 mg sodium.

Lemon Cornmeal Thins

Grated lemon peel ensures lots of piquant flavor. Similar to an Italian recipe called *zaleti*, these cookies are made with cornmeal, so they're nice and crunchy.

PREP: 30 MINUTES PLUS CHILLING   BAKE: 16 MINUTES PER BATCH
MAKES ABOUT 56 COOKIES

3/4 cup butter or margarine (1 1/2 sticks), softened
1 cup sugar
2 large eggs
1 tablespoon freshly grated lemon peel

2 teaspoons vanilla extract
1 1/2 cups all-purpose flour
1 1/2 cups yellow cornmeal
3/4 teaspoon baking powder
1/2 teaspoon salt

1. In large bowl, with mixer at medium speed, beat butter and sugar until creamy. Reduce speed to low and beat in eggs, lemon peel, and vanilla (mixture may look curdled). Gradually beat in flour, cornmeal, baking powder, and salt just until dough is evenly moistened.

2. With floured hands, divide dough in half. Shape each half into a 7" by 2" brick. Wrap each brick in plastic and refrigerate overnight, or freeze dough 1 hour. (If using margarine, freeze dough at least 6 hours.)

3. Preheat oven to 350°F. Grease large cookie sheet. With serrated knife, cut 1 brick crosswise into 1/4 -inch-thick slices. Place slices, 1 inch apart, on prepared cookie sheet. Bake until edges are golden, 16 to 18 minutes. With wide metal spatula, transfer cookies to wire rack to cool.

4. Repeat with remaining dough.

Each cookie: about 70 calories, 1 g protein, 9 g carbohydrates, 3 g total fat (2 g saturated), 15 mg cholesterol, 55 mg sodium.

Spicy Almond Slices

The spicy aroma of these almond cookies baking is so welcoming that family and guests will head for the kitchen to see what's for dessert.

PREP: 25 MINUTES PLUS CHILLING   BAKE: 10 MINUTES PER BATCH
MAKES ABOUT 80 COOKIES

3 1/2 cups all-purpose flour
1 tablespoon ground cinnamon
1 teaspoon baking soda
1/2 teaspoon ground cloves
1/2 teaspoon ground nutmeg
1/2 teaspoon salt
1 cup butter or margarine (2 sticks), softened

1 cup granulated sugar
3/4 cup packed dark brown sugar
2 large eggs
1 teaspoon vanilla extract
2 cups sliced blanched almonds (8 ounces)

1. In medium bowl, combine flour, cinnamon, baking soda, cloves, nutmeg, and salt. In large bowl, with mixer at medium speed, beat butter and granulated and brown sugars until light and fluffy. Beat in eggs, one at a time; add vanilla. Reduce speed to low; beat in flour mixture just until blended. With wooden spoon, stir in almonds (dough will be stiff).

2. Divide dough in half. Shape each half into 10" by 3" by 1" rectangle; wrap each piece in plastic and refrigerate overnight, or freeze until very firm, at least 2 hours.

3. Preheat oven to 375°F. Cut 1 rectangle crosswise into 1/4-inch-thick slices; keep remaining dough refrigerated. Place slices, 1 inch apart, on two ungreased cookie sheets. Bake until edges are browned, 10 to 12 minutes, rotating cookie sheets between upper and lower oven racks halfway through baking. With wide metal spatula, transfer cookies to wire racks to cool completely.

4. Repeat with remaining dough.

Each cookie: About 79 calories, 1 g protein, 9 g carbohydrate, 4 g total fat (2 g saturated), 12 mg cholesterol, 58 mg sodium.

Almond Refrigerator Cookies

With this nut-flavored dough in the freezer, you are never more than fifteen minutes away from fresh homemade cookies.

PREP: 25 MINUTES PLUS CHILLING   BAKE: 15 MINUTES PER BATCH
MAKES 32 COOKIES

1 1/3 cups all-purpose flour	2 large eggs
2 teaspoons baking powder	1/2 teaspoon vanilla extract
1/4 teaspoon salt	1/4 teaspoon almond extract
1/2 cup butter or margarine (1 stick), softened	1 tablespoon water
	32 whole blanched almonds
3/4 cup sugar	

1. In small bowl, stir together flour, baking powder, and salt. In large bowl, with mixer at medium speed, beat butter and sugar until creamy. Beat in 1 egg and vanilla and almond extracts until blended. Reduce speed to low and beat in flour mixture just until combined, scraping bowl with rubber spatula.

2. On sheet of waxed paper, shape dough into 8" by 1 1/2" log. Wrap in waxed paper and refrigerate until firm enough to slice, 2 hours. (If using margarine, freeze overnight.)

3. Preheat oven to 350°F. Cut log crosswise into 1/4-inch-thick slices. Place slices, 1 inch apart, on ungreased large cookie sheet. Whisk together remaining egg and water. Brush cookies with egg glaze. Lightly press 1 almond into the center of each cookie. Bake until lightly browned, 15 minutes. With wide metal spatula, transfer to wire racks to cool completely.

4. Repeat with remaining dough and almonds.

Each cookie: About 80 calories, 1 g protein, 10 g carbohydrate, 4 g total fat (2 g saturated), 22 mg cholesterol, 85 mg sodium.

Chocolate Refrigerator Cookies

You can serve these versatile cookies plain, decorate them with frosting, or make a cookie sandwich filled with jam or melted white chocolate. Crushed, they make a great crust for chocolate cream pie.

PREP: 25 MINUTES PLUS CHILLING   BAKE: 10 MINUTES PER BATCH
MAKES ABOUT 96 COOKIES

1 2/3 cups all-purpose flour
1/2 cup unsweetened cocoa
1 teaspoon baking powder
1/2 teaspoon baking soda
1/4 teaspoon salt
3/4 cup butter or margarine
   (1 1/2 sticks), softened

1/2 cup packed light brown sugar
1/2 cup granulated sugar
2 squares (2 ounces) semisweet
   chocolate, melted and cooled
1 teaspoon vanilla extract
1 large egg

1. In medium bowl, stir together flour, cocoa, baking powder, baking soda, and salt.

2. In large bowl, with mixer at medium speed, beat butter and brown and granulated sugars until light and fluffy. Beat in chocolate and vanilla until well combined. Beat in egg. Reduce speed to low and beat in flour mixture until well combined.

3. Divide dough in half. On separate sheets of waxed paper, shape each half into 12" by 1 1/2" log. Wrap each log in the waxed paper and slide onto small cookie sheet for easier handling. Refrigerate dough until firm enough to slice, at least 2 hours or overnight. (If using margarine, freeze overnight.)

4. Preheat oven to 350°F. Cut 1 log crosswise into scant 1/4-inch-thick slices; keep remaining log refrigerated. Place slices, 1 inch apart, on two ungreased large cookie sheets. Bake until firm, 10 to 11 minutes, rotating sheets between upper and lower oven racks halfway through baking. Cool on cookie sheets on wire racks 1 minute. With wide metal spatula, transfer to wire racks to cool completely.

5. Repeat with remaining dough.

Each cookie: About 44 calories, 0 g protein, 5 g carbohydrate, 3 g total fat (1 g saturated), 6 mg cholesterol, 31 mg sodium.

Lime Refrigerator Cookies

The refreshing flavor of lime creates a delicate cookie. Shaping the dough into rectangles before chilling makes them easier to slice because they rest flat on the cutting board, and they don't lose their shape from the pressure of the knife.

PREP: 30 MINUTES PLUS CHILLING   BAKE: 12 MINUTES PER BATCH
MAKES ABOUT 48 COOKIES

3 limes	1 large egg
1/2 cup butter or margarine	1 3/4 cups all-purpose flour
(1 stick), softened	about 1/2 cup confectioners' sugar
3/4 cup granulated sugar	

1. From limes, grate 1 teaspoon peel and squeeze 3 tablespoons juice. In medium bowl, with mixer at medium speed, beat butter and granulated sugar until creamy. Reduce speed to low; beat in egg and lime peel and juice until blended. Beat in flour until combined.

2. Divide dough in half. On separate sheets of waxed paper, shape each half into 6" by 2 1/2" by 1 1/2" brick. Wrap each brick in the waxed paper and freeze 3 hours or up to 1 month.

3. Preheat oven to 350°F. Slice 1 brick crosswise into 1/4-inch-thick slices. Place slices, 1 inch apart, on ungreased large cookie sheet. Bake until edges are golden brown, 12 to 15 minutes. With wide metal spatula, transfer to wire racks. Sift confectioners' sugar over hot cookies.

4. Repeat with remaining dough and confectioners' sugar.

Each cookie: About 50 calories, 1 g protein, 8 g carbohydrate, 2 g total fat (1 g saturated), 10 mg cholesterol, 20 mg sodium.

Oatmeal Refrigerator Cookies

The perfect after-school treat, these crisp oatmeal slices can be decorated with raisin, currant, or chocolate chip happy faces before baking. With a roll or two of these in the freezer, you can slice off and bake just what you need, whenever you want.

PREP: 35 MINUTES PLUS CHILLING   BAKE: 14 MINUTES PER BATCH
MAKES ABOUT 60 COOKIES

1 1/2 cups all-purpose flour
1 teaspoon baking powder
1/2 teaspoon baking soda
1/4 teaspoon salt
1 cup butter or margarine (2 sticks), softened
1 cup packed dark brown sugar

3/4 cup granulated sugar
2 large eggs
2 teaspoons vanilla extract
3 cups old-fashioned oats, uncooked
1 cup pecans
1 cup raisins

1. On sheet of waxed paper, stir together flour, baking powder, baking soda, and salt until blended.

2. In large bowl, with mixer at medium speed, beat butter and brown and granulated sugars until creamy. Beat in eggs, one at a time, until blended. Beat in vanilla. Reduce speed to low and beat in flour mixture until combined. With wooden spoon, stir in oats, pecans, and raisins.

3. Divide dough in half. On separate sheets of waxed paper, shape each half into 12-inch-long log. Wrap each log in the waxed paper and refrigerate 4 hours or overnight, until firm.

4. Preheat oven to 350°F. With serrated knife, using sawing motion, cut each log crosswise into 3/8-inch-thick slices. Place slices, 2 inches apart, on two ungreased large cookie sheets. Bake 14 minutes, rotating sheets between upper and lower racks halfway through baking, until golden brown.

Cool on cookie sheets on wire racks 2 minutes. With wide metal spatula, transfer to wire racks to cool completely.

5. Repeat with remaining cookie dough.

Each cookie: About 100 calories, 1 g protein, 13 g carbohydrate, 5 g total fat (2 g saturated), 15 mg cholesterol, 65 mg sodium.

HOLIDAY COOKIES

Ever since the seventeenth and eighteenth centuries, when sugar and spices were great luxuries, cookies have been associated with festive occasions. Today, sugar and spices are household staples. Even so we usually make these special cookies, many of them beautifully decorated, just once a year, and their spicy aroma is usually the first sign that the holidays are about to begin.

In this chapter, you will find old-world classics, new seasonal ideas from the *Good Housekeeping* kitchens, and many personal favorites from our staff and readers. As you select recipes for your holiday baking, we hope some of them will become a part of your family's tradition.

Celebration cookies make welcome gifts, so they often have to travel. You may want to send boxes to friends across the country, pack tins for hostess gifts, or fill a basket for the folks at the office. Here's how to make sure your cookies arrive in perfect condition.

• *When shipping by mail*, choose chewy, soft drop, or bar cookies, which travel well. Avoid crisp cookies, which are more likely to break.

• *To wrap*, line a sturdy cardboard box or tin with waxed paper or bubble wrap. Wrap the cookies individually or in pairs, back to back, with plastic wrap.

• *Cushion each layer* with crumpled waxed paper, filling any empty spaces with crumpled paper or bubble wrap, and be sure to mark the wrapped package FRAGILE.

• *When packing cookie assortments* for local delivery, pack them as close to the delivery date as possible to reduce the amount of flavor exchange among the cookies.

• *Pack soft and crisp cookies* in separate packages so that each will retain its ideal texture.

Jelly Centers

Ann Marie Reinle of Massapequa, New York, enjoyed these cookies every Christmas at a friend's home. So when her friend moved away, she made sure to ask for the recipe!

PREP: 45 MINUTES PLUS CHILLING AND COOLING
BAKE: 10 MINUTES PER BATCH
MAKES ABOUT 54 SANDWICH COOKIES

1 cup margarine or butter (2 sticks), softened
1 1/4 cups sugar
2 large eggs, separated
2 teaspoons vanilla extract
3 cups all-purpose flour
1/8 teaspoon baking powder
1/8 teaspoon salt
about 1 cup seedless raspberry preserves

1. In large bowl, with mixer at low speed, beat margarine and 1 cup sugar until blended, occasionally scraping bowl with rubber spatula. Increase speed to high; beat until light and fluffy, about 3 minutes. At low speed, beat in egg yolks and vanilla until blended. Gradually beat in flour, baking powder, and salt. Shape dough into 2 balls; flatten each slightly. Wrap each ball in plastic and refrigerate until firm enough to roll, 1 hour.

2. Preheat oven to 350°F. Between two sheets of floured waxed paper, roll 1 piece of dough 1/8 inch thick; keep remaining dough refrigerated. With floured 2-inch cookie cutter (we like rounds or stars), cut out as many cookies as possible. Place cookies, about 1/2 inch apart, on ungreased large cookie sheet; reserve trimmings. With 1/2-inch round or star-shaped cookie cutter, cut out centers from half of cookies. Remove centers; add to trimmings.

3. In cup, with fork, beat egg whites slightly. With pastry brush, brush cookies with cut-out centers with some egg white, then sprinkle with some of remaining 1/4 cup sugar. Bake all cookies until lightly browned, 10 to 12 minutes. With wide metal spatula, transfer cookies to wire rack to cool.

4. Repeat Steps 2 and 3 with trimmings and remaining dough.

5. When cookies are cool, spread center of each cookie without cut-out center with 1/4 to 1/2 teaspoon preserves; top each with a cookie with a cut-out center, gently pressing cookies together to form a sandwich.

Each cookie: About 95 calories, 1 g protein, 14 g carbohydrate, 4 g total fat (1 g saturated), 8 mg cholesterol, 55 mg sodium.

Old-Time Spice Cookies

Shirley A. Fisher of Bethlehem, Pennsylvania, told us that her family enjoys these cut-out cookies for every holiday: Valentine's Day, Easter, even the Fourth of July. The recipe dates to the late 1890s and was handed down by her great-grandmother.

PREP: 1 HOUR 10 MINUTES PLUS CHILLING, COOLING, AND DECORATING
BAKE: 8 MINUTES PER BATCH
MAKES ABOUT 48 COOKIES

5 1/2 cups all-purpose flour
1 teaspoon ground cinnamon
1 teaspoon ground allspice
1/2 teaspoon ground nutmeg
1/2 teaspoon baking soda
1/2 teaspoon salt

1 cup margarine or butter (2 sticks), softened
1 1/4 cups packed light brown sugar
1 jar (12 ounces) dark molasses
Ornamental Frosting (see page 248; optional)

1. In large bowl, combine flour, cinnamon, allspice, nutmeg, baking soda, and salt. In separate large bowl, with mixer at low speed, beat margarine and brown sugar until blended. Increase speed to high; beat until light and creamy. At low speed, beat in molasses until blended, then beat in 3 cups flour mixture. With spoon, stir in remaining flour mixture. Divide dough into 4 equal pieces. Wrap each piece in plastic and freeze until dough is firm enough to roll, at least 1 hour or refrigerate overnight.

2. Preheat oven to 350°F. On well-floured surface, with floured rolling pin, roll 1 piece of dough 1/8 inch thick; keep remaining dough refrigerated (dough will be soft). With floured 3- to 4-inch assorted cookie cutters, cut dough into as many cookies as possible; reserve trimmings. Place cookies, about 1 inch apart, on ungreased large cookie sheet.

3. Bake until just browned, 8 to 10 minutes. Cool cookies on cookie sheet on wire rack 5 minutes. With wide metal spatula, transfer cookies to wire rack to cool completely. Repeat with remaining dough and reserved trimmings.

4. When cookies are cool, if you like, prepare Ornamental Frosting. Use to decorate cookies as desired. Set cookies aside to allow frosting to dry completely, about 1 hour.

Each cookie without frosting: About 120 calories, 2 g protein, 21 g carbohydrate, 4 g total fat (1 g saturated), 0 mg cholesterol, 95 mg sodium.

Sand Tarts

Pennsylvania bakers used to compete to see who could make the thinnest, crispest sand tarts. *Good Housekeeping* reader Vivian A. Eck of Williamsport, Pennsylvania, sent us this traditional recipe, which has been in her family for five generations.

PREP: 1 HOUR 30 MINUTES PLUS CHILLING, COOLING, AND DECORATING
BAKE: 12 MINUTES PER BATCH
MAKES ABOUT 72 COOKIES

1 cup butter (2 sticks), softened
   (do not use margarine)
1 1/2 cups sugar
2 large eggs
1 teaspoon vanilla extract

3 cups all-purpose flour
1/2 teaspoon baking powder
1/2 teaspoon salt
Ornamental Frosting (see page 248;
   optional)

1. In large bowl, with mixer at low speed, beat butter and sugar until blended. Increase speed to high; beat until light and creamy. At low speed, beat in eggs and vanilla until mixed. Beat in flour, baking powder, and salt until well combined, occasionally scraping bowl with rubber spatula. Shape dough into 4 balls; flatten each slightly. Wrap each ball of dough in plastic wrap and freeze until dough is firm enough to roll, at least 1 hour or refrigerate overnight.

2. Preheat oven to 350°F. On lightly floured surface, with floured rolling pin, roll 1 piece of dough slightly thinner than 1/4 inch; keep remaining dough refrigerated. With floured 3- to 4-inch assorted cookie cutters, cut dough into as many cookies as possible; reserve trimmings. Place cookies, about 1 inch apart, on ungreased large cookie sheet.

3. Bake until edges are golden, 12 to 15 minutes. With wide metal spatula, transfer cookies to wire rack to cool. Repeat with remaining dough and trimmings.

4. When cookies are cool, if you like, prepare Ornamental Frosting. Use to decorate cookies as desired. Set cookies aside to allow frosting to dry completely, about 1 hour.

Each cookie without frosting: About 60 calories, 1 g protein, 8 g carbohydrate, 3 g total fat (2 g saturated), 13 mg cholesterol, 45 mg sodium.

Angeletti

These luscious glazed cookies came to us from freelance home economist Marjorie Cubisino, who got them from "the best cook I ever met!"—her mother-in-law, Carmel.

PREP: 40 MINUTES PLUS COOLING   BAKE: 7 MINUTES PER BATCH
MAKES ABOUT 60 COOKIES

1/2 cup butter or margarine (1 stick), melted
3/4 cup granulated sugar
1/4 cup whole milk
1 1/2 teaspoons vanilla extract
3 large eggs
3 cups all-purpose flour

1 tablespoon baking powder
1/4 teaspoon salt
2 cups confectioners' sugar
3 tablespoons plus 1 1/2 teaspoons water
1/2 cup multicolor candy décors

1. Preheat oven to 375°F. Grease large cookie sheet.

2. In large bowl, whisk butter, granulated sugar, milk, vanilla, and eggs until blended. In medium bowl, mix flour, baking powder, and salt. Stir flour mixture into egg mixture until evenly blended. Cover dough with plastic wrap or waxed paper; let stand 5 minutes.

3. With floured hands, shape dough by level tablespoons into 1-inch balls. Place balls, 2 inches apart, on prepared cookie sheet. Bake until puffed and light brown on bottoms, 7 to 8 minutes. With wide metal spatula, transfer cookies to wire rack to cool. Repeat with remaining dough.

4. When cookies are cool, in small bowl, whisk confectioners' sugar and water until blended. Dip top of each cookie into glaze. Place cookies on wire rack set over waxed paper to catch any drips. Immediately sprinkle cookies with décors. Allow glaze to set, about 20 minutes.

Each cookie: About 75 calories, 1 g protein, 13 g carbohydrate, 2 g total fat (1 g saturated), 15 mg cholesterol, 55 mg sodium.

Christmas Rocks

Betty Pfeifer of Bay Village, Ohio, discovered this recipe in her high school cooking class. She has been making them ever since, changing nothing but the kind of candied fruit she uses.

PREP: 45 MINUTES   BAKE: 12 MINUTES PER BATCH
MAKES ABOUT 48 COOKIES

1/2 cup packed light brown sugar
1/3 cup shortening
6 tablespoons margarine or butter (3/4 stick), softened
2 large eggs
1 1/2 cups all-purpose flour
1 teaspoon baking powder
1 teaspoon ground cinnamon
1/2 teaspoon baking soda

1/2 teaspoon salt
1/4 teaspoon ground cloves
2 cups walnuts, coarsely chopped
2 cups dark seedless raisins
1/2 cup dried currants
1/2 cup red and/or green candied cherries, each cut in half
1/2 cup diced candied pineapple

1. In large bowl, with mixer at low speed, beat brown sugar, shortening, and margarine until mixed, occasionally scraping bowl with rubber spatula. Increase speed to high; beat mixture until creamy, about 2 minutes. Reduce speed to low and beat in eggs. Beat in flour, baking powder, cinnamon, baking soda, salt, and cloves just until mixed. With wooden spoon, stir in walnuts, raisins, currants, cherries, and pineapple.
2. Preheat oven to 350°F. Drop dough by rounded tablespoons, about 1 1/2 inches apart, on ungreased large cookie sheet. Bake until set and lightly browned, 12 to 15 minutes. With wide metal spatula, transfer cookies to wire rack to cool.
3. Repeat with remaining dough.

Each cookie: About 120 calories, 2 g protein, 16 g carbohydrate, 6 g total fat (1 g saturated), 9 mg cholesterol, 70 mg sodium.

Grandma's Rolled Crescents

Mary Charney brought this Christmas cookie recipe with her when she came to America from the Ukraine in 1910. Eventually she gave it to her granddaughter, Lee Quarfoot, who gave it to us. The versatile cookie can be filled with any fruit preserves or with almond paste instead of prune butter.

PREP: 1 HOUR 15 MINUTES PLUS CHILLING
BAKE: 25 MINUTES PER BATCH
MAKES 48 COOKIES

1 cup walnuts, toasted
   (see page 73)
1/2 cup plus 2 tablespoons
   granulated sugar
3 1/4 cups all-purpose flour
2 1/2 teaspoons baking powder
1/2 teaspoon salt
1 cup cold butter (2 sticks), cut into
   pieces (do not use margarine)

2 large eggs
1 teaspoon almond extract
1/3 cup plus 2 tablespoons milk
1 jar (17 ounces) prune butter
   (lekvar; about 1 1/2 cups)
confectioners' sugar

1. In food processor with knife blade attached, process walnuts and 1/4 cup granulated sugar until nuts are finely ground. Add flour, baking powder, and salt; pulse until blended. Add butter and pulse until coarse crumbs form. Add eggs, almond extract, and 1/3 cup milk and pulse until dough just begins to form and pulls away from side of work bowl. Gather dough together and pat into a ball. Divide dough into 6 equal pieces. Wrap each piece with plastic and refrigerate until firm enough to roll, at least 2 hours or overnight.

2. Preheat oven to 350°F. In medium bowl, mix prune butter and 1/4 cup granulated sugar. Grease two large cookie sheets.

3. On floured surface, with floured rolling pin, roll 1 piece of chilled dough into a 9-inch round; keep remaining dough refrigerated. Spread dough with 1/4 cup prune mixture. With pastry wheel or sharp knife, cut dough into 8 equal wedges. Starting at curved edge, roll up each wedge, jelly-roll fashion. Place cookies, pointed end down, 2 inches apart, on prepared cookie sheet. Repeat with 2 more pieces of dough.

4. With pastry brush, brush crescents with 1 tablespoon milk, then sprinkle with 1 tablespoon granulated sugar.

5. Bake crescents until golden, 25 minutes, rotating cookie sheets between upper and lower oven racks halfway through baking time. Immediately transfer crescents to wire rack to cool.

6. Repeat with remaining 3 pieces of dough. Sprinkle with confectioners' sugar before serving.

Each cookie: About 110 calories, 2 g protein, 13 g carbohydrate, 6 g total fat (3 g saturated), 19 mg cholesterol, 105 mg sodium.

Cream Cheese–Walnut Cookies

These rich cookies are made with just six ingredients! You can decorate them with colored sugar or sprinkles.

PREP: 30 MINUTES   BAKE: 14 MINUTES PER BATCH
MAKES ABOUT 60 COOKIES

1/2 cup margarine or butter (1 stick), softened	1 cup sugar
	1 teaspoon vanilla extract
1 package (3 ounces) cream cheese, softened	1 cup all-purpose flour
	1/2 cup walnuts, finely chopped

1. Preheat oven to 350°F. In large bowl, with mixer at low speed, beat margarine, cream cheese, and sugar until blended. Increase speed to high; beat until creamy, about 2 minutes, scraping bowl with rubber spatula. Beat in vanilla. With wooden spoon, stir in flour and walnuts just until blended.

2. With lightly floured hands, roll dough into 1-inch balls. Place balls, 2 inches apart, on ungreased large cookie sheet. With floured fingertips, flatten balls into 1 1/4-inch rounds. Bake until golden, 14 to 18 minutes. Let cool on cookie sheet on wire rack 2 minutes. With wide metal spatula, transfer cookies to wire rack to cool completely.

3. Repeat with remaining dough.

Each cookie: About 45 calories, 1 g protein, 5 g carbohydrate, 3 g total fat (1 g saturated), 2 mg cholesterol, 25 mg sodium.

Cuccidati

The almond filling for these Sicilian Christmas cookies is flavored with orange, lemon, and cinnamon, then slowly simmered. Tony Arena gave us his mother's heirloom family recipe.

PREP: 1 HOUR   BAKE: 18 MINUTES PER BATCH

MAKES 64 COOKIES

ALMOND FILLING
1 1/2 cups blanched whole almonds
   (8 ounces)
1 cup sugar
1 cup water
2 strips (3" by 1" each) fresh
   orange peel
1 strip (3" by 1") fresh lemon peel
1/4 teaspoon ground cinnamon

DOUGH
2 1/4 cups all-purpose flour
1/2 cup sugar

(Dough—continued)
2 teaspoons baking powder
4 tablespoons cold margarine or butter
   (1/2 stick), cut into pieces
1/4 cup vegetable shortening
1/4 cup milk
1 large egg
1 1/2 teaspoons freshly grated
   orange peel
confectioners' sugar for garnish

1. Prepare filling: In food processor with knife blade attached, process almonds and sugar until almonds are very finely ground. Pour mixture into 2-quart saucepan. Add water, orange and lemon peels, and cinnamon; heat almond mixture to boiling over medium-high heat, stirring occasionally. Reduce heat to medium-low and simmer, stirring occasionally, until mixture is thick, about 45 minutes. Discard citrus peels. Set mixture aside to cool.

2. Meanwhile, prepare dough: In large bowl, combine flour, sugar, and baking powder. With pastry blender or two knives used scissor-fashion, cut in margarine and shortening until mixture resembles fine crumbs. With fork, stir in milk, egg, and grated orange peel. With hands, knead flour mixture in bowl until dough forms; shape into a ball. Divide dough into 4 equal pieces.

3. Preheat oven to 375°F. Grease large cookie sheet. On floured surface, with floured rolling pin, roll 1 piece of dough into 12" by 5" rectangle. With moist fingertips, spread one-fourth almond mixture in 2-inch-wide lengthwise strip down center of dough, leaving 1/2-inch border at each

end. Fold long sides of dough over filling, slightly overlapping; press gently to seal. With floured wide metal spatula, transfer log, seam side down, to lightly floured cutting board; cut crosswise into 16 slices. Place slices, 2 inches apart, on cookie sheet.

4. Bake until lightly browned, 18 to 20 minutes. Transfer cookies to wire rack to cool completely.

5. Repeat with remaining dough and filling. Sprinkle with confectioners' sugar to serve.

Each cookie: About 75 calories, 2 g protein, 10 g carbohydrate, 4 g total fat (1 g saturated), 4 mg cholesterol, 25 mg sodium.

Coconut Macaroons

A traditional Passover sweet, these flourless cookies are delicious any time of the year (and a welcome treat to people who are allergic to wheat or gluten).

PREP: 10 MINUTES   BAKE: 25 MINUTES
MAKES ABOUT 42 COOKIES

3 cups flaked sweetened coconut	1/4 teaspoon salt
3/4 cup sugar	1 teaspoon vanilla extract
4 large egg whites	1/8 teaspoon almond extract

1. Preheat oven to 325°F. Line two cookie sheets with cooking parchment or foil.

2. In large bowl, stir coconut, sugar, egg whites, salt, vanilla, and almond extract until well combined.

3. Drop batter by rounded teaspoons, 1 inch apart, on prepared cookie sheets. Bake until set and lightly golden, about 25 minutes, rotating cookie sheets between upper and lower oven racks halfway through baking. Cool 1 minute on cookie sheets. With wide metal spatula, transfer cookies to wire racks to cool completely.

Each cookie: About 41 calories, 1 g protein, 6 g carbohydrate, 2 g total fat (2 g saturated), 0 mg cholesterol, 32 mg sodium.

Chocolate Coconut Macaroons: Prepare as directed, stirring *2 tablespoons unsweetened cocoa* and *1 square (1 ounce) semisweet chocolate,* grated, into coconut mixture.

Greek Christmas Cookies

Diane Sanchez of Auburndale, Florida, told us that her family has been making these colorful spice cookies for Christmas for at least forty years.

PREP: 50 MINUTES   BAKE: 15 MINUTES PER BATCH
MAKES ABOUT 72 COOKIES

1 cup margarine or butter
  (2 sticks), softened
2 cups confectioners' sugar
2 cups all-purpose flour
1 teaspoon ground cinnamon
1/2 teaspoon ground nutmeg

1/2 teaspoon ground cloves
1/8 teaspoon salt
1 large egg yolk
2 cups blanched almonds, ground
about 1 cup red candied cherries,
  each cut in half

1. Preheat oven to 350°F. In large bowl, with mixer at low speed, beat margarine and confectioners' sugar until blended. Increase speed to high; beat until light and creamy. At low speed, beat in flour, cinnamon, nutmeg, cloves, salt, and egg yolk. With hands, knead in almonds.

2. Roll dough into 1-inch balls (dough will be crumbly). Place balls, about 2 inches apart, on ungreased large cookie sheet. Gently press a cherry half on top of each ball. Bake until bottoms of cookies are lightly browned, 15 minutes. With wide metal spatula, transfer cookies to wire rack to cool.

3. Repeat with remaining dough and cherries.

Each cookie: About 75 calories, 1 g protein, 9 g carbohydrate, 4 g total fat (1 g saturated), 3 mg cholesterol, 40 mg sodium.

Czechoslovakian Cookies

Barbara Karpinski of Somerset, New Jersey, was given the recipe for these traditional Christmas cookies by her mother-in-law. Kids will love assembling the strawberry and walnut layers in the baking pan.

PREP: 25 MINUTES   BAKE: 45 MINUTES
MAKES 30 BARS

1 cup butter (2 sticks), softened   2 cups all-purpose flour
   (do not use margarine)   1/8 teaspoon salt
1 cup sugar   1 cup walnuts, chopped
2 large egg yolks   1/2 cup strawberry preserves

1. Preheat oven to 350°F. Grease 9-inch square baking pan.

2. In large bowl, with mixer at low speed, beat butter and sugar until mixed, occasionally scraping bowl with rubber spatula. Increase speed to high; beat until light and fluffy. Reduce speed to low and beat in egg yolks until well combined, constantly scraping bowl with rubber spatula. Add flour and salt and beat until blended, occasionally scraping bowl. With wooden spoon, stir in chopped walnuts.

3. With lightly floured hands, divide dough in half. Pat 1 piece of dough evenly into bottom of prepared pan. Spread strawberry preserves over dough. With lightly floured hands, pinch off 3/4-inch pieces from remaining dough and drop over preserves; do not pat down.

4. Bake until golden, 45 to 50 minutes. Cool completely in pan on wire rack. When cool, cut lengthwise into 3 strips, then cut each strip crosswise into 10 pieces.

Each bar: About 130 calories, 2 g protein, 11 g carbohydrate, 9 g total fat (4 g saturated), 31 mg cholesterol, 70 mg sodium.

Clockwise from top right: Wooden-Spoon Cookies (page 246), Hazelnut Cookies (page 224), Czechoslovakian Cookies (opposite)

Hazelnut Cookies

Susan Willey Spalt learned to make these hazelnut meringues from her mother. The recipe came along with her mom's reminder that the baking can't be hurried.

PREP: 1 HOUR PLUS COOLING   BAKE: 25 MINUTES PER BATCH
MAKES ABOUT 48 SANDWICH COOKIES

2 cups hazelnuts (filberts)	5 tablespoons margarine or butter,
3/4 cup sugar	melted and cooled
5 large egg whites	6 squares (6 ounces) semisweet
1/3 cup all-purpose flour	chocolate, melted and cooled

1. Preheat oven to 350°F. Toast and skin hazelnuts (see page 73).

2. Turn oven control to 275°F. Grease two large cookie sheets. In food processor with knife blade attached, process hazelnuts and 1/4 cup sugar until nuts are finely ground.

3. In large bowl, with mixer at high speed, beat egg whites until soft peaks form when beaters are lifted. Increase speed to high and sprinkle in remaining 1/2 cup sugar, 1 tablespoon at a time, beating well after each addition, until sugar has completely dissolved and whites stand in stiff peaks. With rubber spatula, fold in ground hazelnuts, flour, and melted margarine.

4. Drop mixture by rounded teaspoons, about 2 inches apart, on prepared cookie sheets. Bake until cookies are firm and edges are golden, 25 minutes, rotating cookie sheets between upper and lower racks halfway through baking time. With wide metal spatula, transfer to wire racks to cool. Repeat with remaining batter.

5. When cookies are cool, with small metal spatula, spread thin layer of melted chocolate onto flat side of half of cookies. Top with remaining cookies, flat side down, to make sandwiches. Spoon remaining chocolate into small zip-tight plastic bag; snip 1 corner of bag to make small hole. Squeeze thin lines of chocolate over cookies. Let stand until set.

Each sandwich cookie: About 75 calories, 1 g protein, 7 g carbohydrate, 5 g total fat (0 g saturated), 0 mg cholesterol, 25 mg sodium.

Lebkuchen

In Europe, this spicy celebration cookie is often baked on a loop of string so it can be worn as a pendant. We just like to eat them!

PREP: 15 MINUTES PLUS COOLING   BAKE: 30 MINUTES
MAKES 64 BARS

1 box (16 ounces) dark brown sugar
4 large eggs
1 1/2 cups all-purpose flour
1 1/2 teaspoons ground cinnamon
1 teaspoon baking powder
3/4 teaspoon ground cloves

1 cup walnuts, coarsely chopped
1 cup dark seedless raisins or 3/4
   cup diced mixed candied fruit
1/2 cup confectioners' sugar
1 tablespoon fresh lemon juice

1. Preheat oven to 350°F. Grease 13" by 9" baking pan. Line pan with foil, extending foil over short ends; grease foil.

2. In large bowl, with mixer at medium speed, beat brown sugar and eggs until well mixed, about 1 minute, occasionally scraping bowl with rubber spatula. Reduce speed to low; gradually beat in flour, cinnamon, baking powder, and cloves until blended, occasionally scraping bowl. With wooden spoon, stir in walnuts and raisins.

3. Spoon mixture into prepared pan and spread evenly. Bake until edges begin to brown, 30 minutes. Cool completely in pan on wire rack.

4. In medium bowl, mix confectioners' sugar and lemon juice. Drizzle icing over Lebkuchen. Let stand 10 minutes to allow icing to set. Lift foil with pastry out of pan and place on cutting board; peel foil away from sides. Cut lengthwise into 8 strips, then cut each strip crosswise into 8 bars.

Each bar: About 65 calories, 1 g protein, 12 g carbohydrate, 2 g total fat (0 g saturated), 13 mg cholesterol, 15 mg sodium.

Hamantaschen

In Jewish homes, Hamantaschen are served for Purim. The three-cornered pastries can be made with either prune or poppy-seed filling.

PREP: 1 HOUR PLUS CHILLING   BAKE: 12 MINUTES PER BATCH
MAKES ABOUT 42 COOKIES

2 cups all-purpose flour	1 large egg
3/4 teaspoon baking powder	1 large egg yolk
1/8 teaspoon salt	1 teaspoon vanilla extract
1 lemon	1 jar (17 ounces) prune butter
1/2 cup butter or margarine	(lekvar; about 1 1/2 cups)
(1 stick), softened	4 teaspoons packed light
2/3 cup granulated sugar	brown sugar

1. In medium bowl, stir together flour, baking powder, and salt. From lemon, grate 1 teaspoon peel and squeeze 1 teaspoon juice.

2. In large bowl, with mixer at medium speed, beat butter until creamy. Beat in granulated sugar until light and fluffy. Beat in egg, egg yolk, vanilla, and 1/2 teaspoon lemon peel until combined. Reduce speed to low and beat in flour mixture until combined. Divide dough in half. Wrap each half in waxed paper and refrigerate several hours or overnight.

3. Preheat oven to 375°F. Line two large cookie sheets with foil. In small bowl, stir together prune butter, brown sugar, lemon juice, and remaining 1/2 teaspoon lemon peel.

4. On lightly floured surface, with floured rolling pin, roll 1 piece of dough 1/8 inch thick; keep remaining dough refrigerated. With 2 1/2-inch round biscuit cutter, cut 20 rounds; reserve trimmings.

5. Spoon 1 teaspoon prune mixture into center of each round. To make triangular pocket, lift edge of dough at three points and pinch together partially covering filling. Place 1 inch apart on prepared cookie sheets.

6. Bake, 1 sheet at a time, 12 minutes, or until pastries are lightly browned. Cool 1 minute on cookie sheet on wire rack. With wide metal spatula, transfer to wire rack to cool completely.

7. Repeat with remaining dough, trimmings, and filling.

Each cookie: About 95 calories, 1 g protein, 17 g carbohydrate, 2 g total fat (1 g saturated), 16 mg cholesterol, 45 mg sodium.

Forming Hamantaschen

To fill the hamantaschen, spoon 1 teaspoon of the prune butter (lekvar) into the center of each dough round.

To shape the three-cornered "hats," lift the edge of the dough at three points and pinch together, partially covering the filling.

Holiday Stained-Glass Cookies

The crushed hard candy melts in the oven to give these beautiful cookies the look of stained glass. They're pretty enough to be hung on your tree.

PREP: 1 HOUR 20 MINUTES   BAKE: 10 MINUTES PER BATCH
MAKES ABOUT 60 COOKIES

Holiday Sugar Cookie dough (see page 230)

1 package (10 to 12 ounces) hard candy, such as sour balls in assorted colors*

1. Prepare Holiday Sugar Cookies dough through Step 1.
2. While dough is chilling, group candies by color and place in separate heavy-duty zip-tight plastic bags. Place 1 bag on towel-covered work surface. With meat mallet or rolling pin, lightly crush candy into small pieces, being careful not to crush until fine and powdery. Repeat with remaining candy.
3. Preheat oven to 350°F. Roll and cut dough as in Step 2 of Holiday Sugar Cookies, but place cut-out cookies on large foil-lined cookie sheet.
4. With mini cookie cutters, canapé cutters, or knife, cut one or more small shapes from each large cookie; remove small cut-out pieces and reserve for rerolling. Place some crushed candy in cutouts of each cookie. With drinking straw, make a hole in top of each cookie for hanging. Bake until lightly browned, 10 to 12 minutes. Cool cookies completely on cookie sheet on wire rack.
5. Repeat with remaining dough and trimmings.
6. For wreath, tree, or window decorations, tie ribbons or nylon fishing line through hole in each cookie to make loop for hanging.

*Do not use red-and-white–swirled peppermint candies—they won't melt in the oven.

Each cookie: About 90 calories, 1 g protein, 14 g carbohydrate, 4 g total fat (1 g saturated), 7 mg cholesterol, 40 mg sodium.

Holiday Stained-Glass Cookies

Holiday Sugar Cookies

At *Good Housekeeping* we like to use this easy-to-handle dough for any holiday cut-out cookies. It is perfect for the Holiday Stained-Glass Cookies (see page 228).

PREP: 30 MINUTES PLUS CHILLING   BAKE: 10 MINUTES PER BATCH
MAKES ABOUT 42 COOKIES

2 1/4 cups all-purpose flour
1 1/2 teaspoons baking powder
1/4 teaspoon salt
3/4 cup butter or margarine
  (1 1/2 sticks), softened

1 cup sugar
1 large egg
1 tablespoon milk
2 teaspoons freshly grated lemon peel
  or vanilla extract

1. In medium bowl, combine flour, baking powder, and salt. In large bowl, with mixer at medium speed, beat butter and 3/4 cup sugar until light and fluffy. Beat in egg, milk, and lemon peel until well combined. Reduce speed to low; beat in flour mixture just until blended. Shape dough into 2 balls; flatten each into disk. Wrap each disk in plastic and refrigerate at least 2 hours or up to overnight.

2. Preheat oven to 350°F. Grease and flour two large cookie sheets. On lightly floured surface, with floured rolling pin, roll 1 disk of dough 1/8 inch thick; keep remaining dough refrigerated. With floured 3-inch assorted cookie cutters, cut dough into as many cookies as possible; reserve trimmings for rerolling. Place cookies, 1 inch apart, on prepared cookie sheets. If desired, with drinking straw or skewer, make 1/4-inch hole in top of each cookie for hanging. Sprinkle some of remaining 1/4 cup sugar over cookies.

3. Bake until golden, about 10 minutes, rotating cookie sheets between upper and lower oven racks halfway through baking. With wide metal spatula, transfer cookies to wire racks to cool completely.

4. Repeat with remaining dough and trimmings.

Each cookie: About 76 calories, 1 g protein, 10 g carbohydrate, 4 g total fat (2 g saturated), 14 mg cholesterol, 66 mg sodium.

Molasses Lace Rolls

Lisa Brainerd-Burge made these elegant cookies for us. Her family has been making them since the 1950s, when the recipe appeared in *The Ladies of Lake Forest*, a community cookbook.

PREP: 30 MINUTES PLUS COOLING   BAKE: 8 MINUTES PER BATCH
MAKES ABOUT 42 COOKIES

1/2 cup light (mild) molasses
1/2 cup butter (1 stick) (do not use margarine)
1/2 cup sugar

1 cup all-purpose flour
1/2 teaspoon baking powder
1/4 teaspoon baking soda

1. Preheat oven to 350°F. Grease large cookie sheet.

2. In 2-quart saucepan, heat molasses, butter, and sugar to boiling over medium heat, stirring often; boil 1 minute. Remove saucepan from heat; gradually stir in flour, baking powder, and baking soda until combined. Place saucepan in skillet of hot water to keep batter warm.

3. Drop batter by heaping teaspoons, 3 inches apart, onto prepared cookie sheet. (Do not place more than six on cookie sheet because, after baking, cookies must be shaped quickly before hardening.) Bake until lacy and lightly browned, 8 minutes.

4. Cool on cookie sheet on wire rack until cookies are set slightly, about 1 minute. With wide metal spatula, quickly loosen and turn cookies over. Working as quickly as possible, roll cookies one at a time around handle of wooden spoon. (If cookies become too hard to roll, reheat on cookie sheet in oven 1 minute to soften.) As each cookie is shaped, remove from spoon handle; cool on wire rack.

5. Repeat with remaining batter.

Each cookie: About 50 calories, 0 g protein, 7 g carbohydrate, 2 g total fat (1 g saturated), 6 mg cholesterol, 35 mg sodium.

Mostaccioli

Food Director Susan Westmoreland's Grandma Elsie used to bake hundreds of these spicy cocoa cookies every Christmas for friends and family.

PREP: 45 MINUTES PLUS COOLING   BAKE: 7 MINUTES PER BATCH
MAKES ABOUT 60 COOKIES

2 cups all-purpose flour
1/2 cup plus 3 tablespoons unsweetened cocoa, plus more for rolling
1 1/2 teaspoons baking powder
1 teaspoon ground cinnamon
1/4 teaspoon ground cloves
1/4 teaspoon salt
3/4 cup granulated sugar

1/2 cup butter or margarine (1 stick),
  softened
1 large egg
1/2 cup milk
1/4 cup boiling water
1 1/4 cups confectioners' sugar
white candy décors for garnish

1. Preheat oven to 400°F. In medium bowl, combine flour, 1/2 cup cocoa, baking powder, cinnamon, cloves, and salt. In large bowl, with mixer at low speed, beat granulated sugar and butter until blended, occasionally scraping bowl with rubber spatula. Increase speed to high; beat until light and creamy. At low speed, beat in egg. Alternately beat in flour mixture and milk, beginning and ending with flour mixture, just until combined, occasionally scraping bowl.

2. With cocoa-dusted hands, shape dough by level tablespoons into 1-inch balls. Place balls, 2 inches apart, on ungreased large cookie sheet. Bake until puffed, 7 to 9 minutes (they will look dry and slightly cracked). With wide metal spatula, transfer cookies to wire rack to cool. Repeat with remaining dough.

3. When cookies are cool, in small bowl, with wire whisk or fork, gradually mix boiling water into remaining 3 tablespoons cocoa until smooth. Gradually stir in confectioners' sugar and blend well. Dip top of each cookie into glaze. Place cookies on wire rack set over waxed paper to catch any drips. Immediately sprinkle cookies with décors. Allow glaze to set, about 20 minutes.

Each cookie: About 55 calories, 1 g protein, 9 g carbohydrate, 2 g total fat (1 g saturated), 8 mg cholesterol, 40 mg sodium.

Pizzelles

Using her grandma's recipe, special large turquoise bowl, and antique pizzelle iron, Jill Sieracki makes these crisp Italian treats each year with her mother and aunt.

PREP: 30 MINUTES PLUS COOLING   BAKE: ABOUT 1 MINUTE PER BATCH
MAKES ABOUT 30 COOKIES

3/4 cup sugar
1/2 cup butter or margarine (1 stick),
  softened
3 large eggs

2 teaspoons vanilla extract
1 3/4 cups all-purpose flour
1 teaspoon baking powder

1. Preheat pizzelle iron (see Note) as manufacturer directs. In large bowl, with mixer at medium speed, beat sugar and butter until creamy. Reduce speed to low; beat in eggs and vanilla until blended. Beat in flour and baking powder just until well mixed, occasionally scraping bowl with rubber spatula.

2. Pour 1 rounded tablespoon batter at a time onto center of each pizzelle mold. Cover and bake as manufacturer directs (do not lift cover during baking). When done, lift cover and loosen pizzelle with fork. Transfer to wire rack to cool completely. Trim cookie edges with scissors if necessary.

3. Repeat with remaining batter.

Note: Pizzelle irons are available in electric and stovetop models in various sizes. Be sure to follow manufacturer's directions for using the correct amount of batter in your iron.

Each cookie: About 60 calories, 1 g protein, 11 g carbohydrate, 4 g total fat (2 g saturated), 30 mg cholesterol, 55 mg sodium.

Nut Crescents

There are many variations of these buttery, ground-nut cookies. Lightly toasting the almonds or hazelnuts intensifies the nutty flavor

PREP: 45 MINUTES PLUS CHILLING   BAKE: 20 MINUTES PER BATCH
MAKES ABOUT 72 COOKIES

1 cup blanched whole almonds or
   hazelnuts (filberts), lightly toasted
   (see page 73)
1/2 cup granulated sugar
1/4 teaspoon salt
1 cup butter (2 sticks),
   softened (do not use margarine)

2 cups all-purpose flour
1 teaspoon almond extract
1/2 teaspoon vanilla extract
3/4 cup confectioners' sugar

1. In food processor with knife blade attached, process almonds, 1/4 cup granulated sugar, and salt until almonds are very finely ground.

2. In large bowl, with mixer at low speed, beat butter and remaining 1/4 cup granulated sugar until blended, occasionally scraping bowl with rubber spatula. Increase speed to high; beat until light and fluffy, about 3 minutes. Reduce speed to low. Gradually add flour, ground-almond mixture, and almond and vanilla extracts; beat until blended. Divide dough in half. Wrap each piece in plastic and refrigerate until dough is firm enough to handle, about 1 hour, or freeze about 30 minutes.

3. Preheat oven to 325°F. Working with 1 piece of dough at a time, with lightly floured hands, shape rounded teaspoons of dough into 2" by 1/2" crescents. Place crescents, 1 inch apart, on two ungreased cookie sheets.

4. Bake until edges are lightly browned, about 20 minutes, rotating cookie sheets between upper and lower oven racks halfway through baking. With wide metal spatula, transfer cookies to wire racks set over waxed paper. Immediately dust confectioners' sugar over cookies until well coated; cool completely.

5. Repeat with remaining dough.

Each cookie: About 58 calories, 1 g protein, 6 g carbohydrate, 4 g total fat (2 g saturated), 7 mg cholesterol, 34 mg sodium.

Nut Crescents

Palmiers

These crisp, flaky pastries are a snap with our easy four-ingredient recipe. The dough can be completely shaped ahead and refrigerated for up to one week or frozen for up to three. Then simply slice and bake the palmiers when you need them.

PREP: 35 MINUTES PLUS CHILLING   BAKE: 15 MINUTES PER BATCH
MAKES ABOUT 112 COOKIES

1 1/2 cups butter (3 sticks), cut into   3/4 cup sour cream
   pieces (do not use margarine)   1 cup sugar
3 cups all-purpose flour

1. In large bowl, with pastry blender or two knives used scissor-fashion, cut butter into flour until mixture resembles coarse crumbs. Stir in sour cream. On lightly floured surface, knead dough just until it holds together; flatten into 8" by 6" rectangle. Wrap in plastic wrap and refrigerate overnight.

2. Preheat oven to 400°F. Sprinkle 1/2 cup sugar evenly over work surface. Cut dough in half. With lightly floured rolling pin, on sugared surface, roll 1 piece of dough into 14-inch square; keep remaining dough refrigerated. Using side of your hand, make indentation down along center of dough. Starting from one side, tightly roll dough up to indentation. Roll up other side of dough until it meets first roll, incorporating as much sugar as possible into dough; refrigerate. Repeat with remaining piece of dough and remaining 1/2 cup sugar.

3. With serrated knife, cut dough scroll crosswise into 1/4-inch-thick slices. (Refrigerate if too soft to slice.) Place slices, 2 inches apart, on ungreased cookie sheet. Bake 10 minutes. With wide metal spatula, carefully turn cookies over and bake until sugar has caramelized and cookies are a deep golden color, about 5 minutes longer. Cool 1 minute on cookie sheet; then, with wide metal spatula, transfer cookies to wire racks to cool completely.

4. Repeat slicing, baking, and cooling with remaining dough scroll.

Each cookie: About 44 calories, 1 g protein, 4 g carbohydrate, 3 g total fat (2 g saturated), 7 mg cholesterol, 26 mg sodium.

ROLLING AND CUTTING PALMIERS

Roll up dough from each side of 14-inch square to meet at a mark in the center. Incorporate as much sugar as possible.

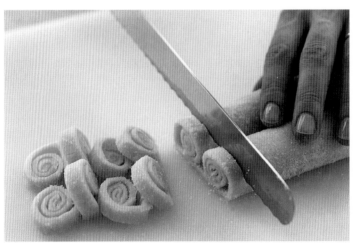

Cut shaped dough crosswise into $1/4$-inch-thick slices with a serrated knife. If the dough seems soft, chill it before cutting.

Peppermint Meringues

Be sure to check your oven temperature before baking these delicately striped meringues. It essential to bake them slowly so that they become crisp inside without browning on the outside.

PREP: 15 MINUTES PLUS DRYING   BAKE: 2 HOURS
MAKES ABOUT 54 MERINGUES

4 large egg whites   1/4 teaspoon peppermint extract*
1/4 teaspoon cream of tartar   red and green food coloring
1 cup confectioners' sugar

1. Preheat oven to 225°F. Line two large cookie sheets with foil.

2. In large bowl, with mixer at high speed, beat egg whites and cream of tartar until soft peaks form when beaters are lifted. Gradually sprinkle in sugar, beating until whites stand in stiff, glossy peaks. Beat in peppermint extract.

3. Transfer half of meringue mixture to another bowl. Add enough red food coloring to meringue in one bowl to tint it a pale red. Add enough green food coloring to remaining meringue to tint it a pale green.

4. Spoon red meringue into large zip-tight plastic bag; cut 1/4-inch opening at corner. Repeat with green meringue in separate bag. Fit large decorating bag (we used a 14-inch bag) with basket-weave or large round tip (1/2-inch- or 3/4-inch-diameter opening). Place decorating bag in 2-cup glass measuring cup to stabilize bag; fold top third of bag over top of cup to keep top of bag clean. Simultaneously, squeeze meringues from both plastic bags into decorating bag, filling decorating bag no more than two-thirds full.

5. Pipe meringue onto prepared cookie sheets, leaving 1 inch between each meringue. If using basket-weave tip, pipe meringue into 3- to 4-inch-long pleated ribbons; if using round tip, pipe meringue into 2-inch rounds. Bake meringues 2 hours. Turn oven off. Leave meringues in oven at least 30 minutes or overnight to dry.

6. Let meringues cool completely before removing from foil with wide metal spatula.

*Do not use peppermint extract containing peppermint oil; the meringue mixture will quickly deflate. We had good results using imitation peppermint extract.

Each meringue: About 10 calories, 0 g protein, 2 g carbohydrate, 0 g total fat, 0 mg cholesterol, 5 mg sodium.

Sally Ann Cookies

These wonderful frosted molasses cookies spiked with coffee were available in midwestern grocery stores in the 1960s. This recipe came to us from Sue Riesterer of Manitowoc, Wisconsin. We adapted it to use butter or margarine in place of lard.

PREP: 1 HOUR PLUS FREEZING AND COOLING
BAKE: 15 MINUTES PER BATCH
MAKES ABOUT 144 COOKIES

1 cup margarine or butter (2 sticks), softened
1 1/2 cups sugar
5 1/2 cups all-purpose flour
1 cup light molasses
1/2 cup cold strong coffee
2 teaspoons baking soda

2 teaspoons ground ginger
1/2 teaspoon ground nutmeg
1/2 teaspoon salt
1/4 teaspoon ground cloves
Sally Ann Frosting (see page 242)
holiday décors (optional)

1. In large bowl, with mixer at low speed, beat margarine and sugar until blended. Increase speed to high; beat until creamy. At low speed, beat in flour, molasses, coffee, baking soda, ginger, nutmeg, salt, and cloves until well blended. Cover bowl with plastic wrap and freeze until firm enough to handle, 1 hour.

2. Divide dough into thirds. On lightly floured surface, shape each third into 12-inch-long log. Wrap each log in plastic and freeze until firm enough to slice, at least 4 hours or overnight.

3. Preheat oven to 350°F. Grease large cookie sheet. Cut 1 log crosswise into 1/4-inch-thick slices. Place slices, 1 1/2 inches apart, on prepared cookie sheet. Bake until cookies are set and edges are lightly browned, 15 to 20 minutes. Cool on cookie sheet on wire rack 1 minute. With wide metal spatula, transfer cookies to wire rack to cool completely. Repeat with remaining dough.

4. When cookies are cool, prepare Sally Ann Frosting. With small metal spatula or knife, spread frosting on cookies. If you like, sprinkle cookies with décors. Set cookies aside to allow frosting to dry completely, about 1 hour.

Plenty-of-Peanuts Bars (page 68), Sally Ann Cookies (opposite)

Sally Ann Frosting: In 2-quart saucepan, stir *1 cup sugar* and *1 envelope un-flavored gelatin* until well mixed. Stir in *1 cup cold water;* heat to boiling over high heat. Reduce heat to low; simmer, uncovered, 10 minutes. Into medium bowl, measure *2 cups confectioners' sugar.* With mixer at low speed, gradually add gelatin mixture to confectioners' sugar until blended. Increase speed to high; beat until smooth and fluffy with an easy spreading consistency, about 10 minutes. Beat in *1/2 teaspoon vanilla extract.* Keep bowl covered with plastic wrap to prevent frosting from drying out.

Each cookie without décors: About 55 calories, 0 g protein, 10 g carbohydrate, 1 g total fat (0 g saturated), 0 mg cholesterol, 40 mg sodium.

Spritz Cookies

Making these buttery molded favorites is easy with one of the new cookie presses. You will find cookie patterns for every holiday, and this dough will work for all of them!

PREP: 15 MINUTES   BAKE: 10 MINUTES PER BATCH
MAKES ABOUT 60 COOKIES

1 cup butter or margarine
  (2 sticks), softened
3/4 cup confectioners' sugar
1 teaspoon vanilla extract

1/8 teaspoon almond extract
2 cups all-purpose flour
1/8 teaspoon salt

1. Preheat oven to 350°F. In large bowl, with mixer at medium speed, beat butter and confectioners' sugar until light and fluffy. Beat in vanilla and almond extracts. Reduce speed to low; add flour and salt and beat until well combined.

2. Spoon one-third of dough into cookie press fitted with pattern of choice. Press cookies, 1 inch apart, on two ungreased cookie sheets.

3. Bake until edges are golden brown, 10 to 12 minutes, rotating cookie sheets between upper and lower oven racks halfway through baking. With wide metal spatula, transfer cookies to wire racks to cool completely.

4. Repeat with remaining dough.

Each cookie: About 48 calories, 0 g protein, 5 g carbohydrate, 3 g total fat (2 g saturated), 8 mg cholesterol, 36 mg sodium.

Chocolate Spritz Cookies

Prepare as directed but use *1 cup confectioners' sugar.* Add *2 squares (2 ounces) unsweetened chocolate,* chopped, melted, and cooled, after beating butter and sugar. Makes about 60 cookies.

Almond Spritz Cookies

In food processor with knife blade attached, process *3/4 cup whole natural almonds,* toasted (see page 73), and *1/4 cup confectioners' sugar* until nuts are finely ground. Prepare as directed, using *1/4 teaspoon almond extract* and *2 1/4 cups all-purpose flour.* Add ground almonds. Dough will be quite stiff. Makes about 72 cookies.

Sugar Hearts

Rachel Long Mattox told us that her mother used to bake these cookies on Christmas Eve and deliver them to parishioners of the church where her father was pastor. Their heart shape makes them a good choice for Valentine's Day, too.

PREP: 1 HOUR PLUS CHILLING AND COOLING
BAKE: 12 MINUTES PER BATCH
MAKES ABOUT 78 COOKIES

1 cup butter (2 sticks), softened
   (do not use margarine)
1 1/2 cups confectioners' sugar
1 large egg
1 teaspoon vanilla extract
2 1/2 cups all-purpose flour
1 teaspoon baking soda

1 teaspoon cream of tartar
about 3/4 cup light corn syrup
   (optional)
green, red, and white sugar crystals
   (optional)

1. In large bowl, with mixer at medium speed, beat butter and confectioners' sugar until creamy. Reduce speed to low; beat in egg and vanilla until blended. Beat in flour, baking soda, and cream of tartar until combined, occasionally scraping bowl with rubber spatula.

2. Divide dough in half; flatten each half into a disk. Wrap each disk in plastic wrap and refrigerate until dough is firm enough to roll, 2 hours, or freeze 15 minutes.

3. Preheat oven to 350°F. On floured surface, with floured rolling pin, roll 1 disk of dough 1/4 inch thick; keep remaining dough refrigerated. With floured heart-shaped cookie cutters in various sizes, cut dough into as many cookies as possible; wrap and refrigerate trimmings. Place cookies, 1 inch apart, on ungreased large cookie sheet.

4. Bake until lightly browned, 12 to 14 minutes. With wide metal spatula, transfer cookies to wire rack to cool. Repeat with remaining dough and trimmings.

5. When cookies are cool, decorate with sugar crystals, if you like: In 1-quart saucepan, heat corn syrup to boiling over medium heat, stirring frequently; boil 1 minute, stirring. Brush cookies with corn syrup, then sprinkle or dip into colored sugar crystals. Repeat with remaining cookies. Reheat syrup if it becomes too thick. Allow decoration to dry completely, about 1 hour.

Each cookie without sugar crystals: About 45 calories, 1 g protein, 5 g carbohydrate, 3 g total fat (2 g saturated), 10 mg cholesterol, 45 mg sodium.

Wooden-Spoon Cookies

Cindie David of Lawrenceville, Georgia, got this recipe from her mother-in-law, who got it from her mother. Be sure to bake only a few at a time so you will be able to roll each cookie around the handle of a wooden spoon before the cookies cool.

PREP: 25 MINUTES   BAKE: 5 MINUTES PER BATCH
MAKES ABOUT 36 COOKIES

3/4 cup blanched almonds, ground	1/2 cup sugar
1/2 cup margarine or butter (1 stick), softened	1 tablespoon all-purpose flour
	1 tablespoon heavy or whipping cream

1. Preheat oven to 350°F. Grease and flour two large cookie sheets. In 2-quart saucepan, combine ground almonds, margarine, sugar, flour, and cream. Heat over low heat, stirring occasionally, until butter melts. Keep mixture warm over very low heat.

2. Drop batter by rounded teaspoons, about 3 inches apart, on prepared cookie sheets. (Do not place more than six on each cookie sheet because, after baking, cookies must be shaped quickly before hardening.)

3. Bake until edges are lightly browned and centers are just golden, 5 to 7 minutes, rotating sheets between upper and lower oven racks halfway through baking. Cool on cookie sheets until edges are just set, 30 to 60 seconds. With wide metal spatula or long, flexible metal spatula, flip cookies over quickly so lacy texture will be on outside after rolling. Working as quickly as possible, roll cookies, one at a time, into a cylinder around handle of wooden spoon; transfer to wire rack. (If cookies become too hard to roll, reheat on cookie sheet in oven 1 minute to soften.) As each cookie is shaped, remove from spoon handle; cool on wire rack.

4. Repeat with remaining batter.

Each cookie: About 50 calories, 1 g protein, 3 g carbohydrate, 4 g total fat (1 g saturated), 1 mg cholesterol, 35 mg sodium.

WOODEN SPOON COOKIES

Remove cookies from the sheet and invert. Working as quickly as possible, roll each hot cookie around the handle of a wooden spoon.

Ornamental Frosting

This fluffy frosting is perfect for decorating holiday cookies. The recipe originally called for three raw egg whites, and you can use them if you have pasteurized eggs in your area. We prefer meringue powder, which is sterilized and now available at many supermarkets and baking supply stores.

PREP: 5 MINUTES   MAKES ABOUT 3 CUPS

1 package (16 ounces) $^1/_3$ cup warm water
   confectioners' sugar   assorted food colorings (optional)
3 tablespoons meringue powder

1. In large bowl, with mixer at medium speed, beat confectioners' sugar, meringue powder, and water until stiff and knife drawn through leaves path, about 5 minutes.
2. If desired, tint frosting with food colorings. Keep tightly covered to prevent drying out. With small metal spatula, artist's paintbrushes, or decorating bags with small plain tips, decorate cookies with frosting. (You may need to thin frosting with a little warm water to obtain ideal spreading or piping consistency.)

Each tablespoon: About 39 calories, 0 g protein, 10 g carbohydrate, 0 g total fat, 0 mg cholesterol, 2 mg sodium.

DECORATING WITH ORNAMENTAL FROSTING

To blend colors, pipe rows or dots of colored frosting onto base coat while it is still wet and pull a toothpick through it to a make feathered design or swirls. Wipe toothpick between each line pulled. To make raised designs, allow base coat to dry completely and then pipe decorations onto cookies.

To pipe details, fit pastry bag with small writing tip and fill with stiff, colored frosting. Pipe designs onto cookies and set aside several hours until all frosting is dry and hard. Cookies may then be wrapped in plastic or packed between layers of waxed paper in a tightly covered container.

INDEX

PHOTOGRAPHY CREDITS

Page 2: Mark Thomas
Page 3: Mark Thomas
Page 8: Steven Mark Needham
Page 9: Brian Hagiwara
Page 10: Brian Hagiwara
Page 13: Brian Hagiwara
Page 14: Mary Ellen Bartley
Page 19: Mark Thomas
Page 21: Mark Thomas
Page 25: Mark Thomas
Page 26: Mark Thomas
Page 33: Steven Mark Needham
Page 34: Mark Thomas
Page 39: Mary Ellen Bartley
Page 46: Steven Mark Needham
Page 51: Alan Richardson
Page 62: Mary Ellen Bartley
Page 66: Mark Thomas
Page 72: Mark Thomas
Page 74: Mark Thomas

Page 79: Mark Thomas
Page 85: Mark Thomas
Page 90: Steven Mark Needham
Page 93: Mark Thomas
Page 94: Mark Thomas
Page 98: Steven Mark Needham
Page 101: Rita Maas
Page 108: Mark Thomas
Page 111: Mark Thomas
Page 119: Steven Mark Needham
Page 120: Steven Mark Needham
Page 129: Mark Thomas
Page 132: Steven Mark Needham
Page 138: Steven Mark Needham
Page 143: Mark Thomas
Page 152: Steven Mark Needham

Page 157: Steven Mark Needham
Page 165: Mark Thomas
Page 166: Mark Thomas
Page 171: Steven Mark Needham
Page 178: Steven Mark Needham
Page 183: Brian Hagiwara
Page 191: Steven Mark Needham
Page 197: Mark Thomas
Page 207: Mark Thomas
Page 223: Mark Thomas
Page 227: Mark Thomas
Page 229: Alan Richardson
Page 235: Mark Thomas
Page 237: Mark Thomas
Page 241: Mark Thomas
Page 247: Mark Thomas
Page 249: Mark Thomas